No Matter What:
A Glimpse into the Heart of Adoption

Short Stories, Excerpts and More

Sue Badeau

First Edition

Published by
Helping Hands Press

ISBN: 978-1-62208-545-3

Printed in the United States of America

Introduction

I am delighted that you are reading this sampler of stories related to the theme that every child, no matter their age or circumstance, needs a family for a lifetime. This basic message has been both the calling and passion of my life. Within these pages you will find both true and fictionalized stories that demonstrate the value and blessing of family for young people who have experienced all kinds of traumas in their lives. Being rooted in a family provides the context, environment and opportunity for healing, wholeness and hope for a brighter future. I'd like to take just a moment and introduce you to the stories you will find in this book.

We begin with the true story of Mary, a teen I met when I was barely out of my own teen years. Her story troubled, haunted and stuck with me as I pursued my dreams and with my husband, Hector, built both my career and our family. Reading about Mary will give you an inkling as to *why* I am so passionate about these issues.

Following Mary's story, I invite you to enjoy some fiction. "Never Too Old" is Volume Three in an eight-volume series of short stories set in the fictional town of Sweetland. Volume Three, shared here, is the story of one adoptive family and several youth in foster care and juvenile justice systems. Through fiction, this story will introduce you to many of the common challenges, yearnings, needs and strengths of the most vulnerable young people in our communities and how connecting to a "forever family" can make a world of difference. If you enjoy this story, I hope you will read the other seven stories in the series. Volume Four, "All Things Work Together" by Peggy Blann Phifer also features foster care themes and allows some of the characters from Volume Three to explore new opportunities.

After Sweetland, I take you back to reality by sharing an excerpt from the memoir my husband and I co-authored about our own family journey, "Are We There Yet? The Ultimate Road Trip Adopting and Raising 22 Kids." Yes, you read that right—we have twenty-two children (all adults now). The excerpt I have chosen to share here is one that reinforces the theme of this book—no child is ever too old to need a family. You will read about how our family added a sibling group of six teenagers to our brood. In this chapter, I introduce the concept of a family not only being there for a lifetime, but also being there *no matter what.* I do hope this excerpt will tempt you to read our entire memoir, which you can find in both electronic and paperback versions.

I often share stories like these when I speak to community and church groups, foster and adoptive parent groups, social workers, judges and others at conferences, retreats or training events. Again and again audiences tell me that hearing stories brings the messages about family home in a way that all the data and research doesn't quite capture. But don't be fooled, while each of these stories is unique, they are not uncommon. The data and research do confirm and support the fact that many of the 400,000 children in foster care today have similar stories, hopes, dreams and needs and each one of us can do something to make a difference.

Finally, I close this book with another piece of fiction by sharing with you the first installment in my series, "Roots and Wings at Loonstone Lake." Like the Sweetland series, this one has eight volumes and the themes related to family connections, healing and hope are woven throughout all eight, along with a little mystery, a little romance and some camping fun. I hope you will enjoy this first volume and be intrigued enough to want to continue reading the rest of the series.

I leave you with two of my favorite quotes:

"There are only two lasting bequests we can hope to give our children. One of these is roots; the other, wings." W. Hodding Carter II (Borrowed from the Reverend Henry Ward Beecher.)

"And whoever receives one such child in My name receives Me" Matthew 18:5

*To learn more about her books or to invite Sue to speak at your event, please visit: **www.suebadeau.com***

Table of Contents

"Open Your Mouth"
Speaking UP for the Voiceless

They say you never forget your first love. You also never forget the first person who breaks your heart.

For me, it was not a boy. The first boy I loved, I married. We've had much heartbreak in 34 years together, raising 22 children, burying three, but he wasn't the first to break my heart.

That was Mary, a scared, pregnant 19-year-old girl.

I was 22 when I met Mary. I was a recent bride and newly licensed foster parent. A nurse friend asked me to reach out to Mary, who had been hospitalized after a suicide attempt. She had no family.

I visited Mary, gently getting to know her. She began to share her life story, growing up in foster care, but quickly became confused. She couldn't remember all of the places she'd lived or people she'd been told to call "mom" or "dad." Foster homes blurred together until the cold December morning when she woke up in a group home, expecting a day like any other.

When a staff person knocked on her bedroom door telling her to gather her things because she was moving, she didn't flinch. It was a common occurrence in her life. As they walked toward the front door, she asked, "Where am I going this time?"

He opened the door, looked out upon the snowy winter day and said, "Happy Birthday, Mary! You're 18, you're free of the system now – go anywhere you want."

A year later, she was 19, pregnant and alone.

We cried, hugged and prayed together. I connected her with resources. I'm not sure if her life changed.

But mine was never the same.

With a broken heart, I sank to my knees, sobbing, asking God what I could do to make a difference for all the other Marys – frightened, disconnected and alone.

"Open your mouth for the mute" God said to me, *"For the rights of all the unfortunate. Open your mouth, judge righteously, defend the rights of the afflicted and needy. Proverbs 31: 8-9*

This is why I speak. Dear Mary, I opened my heart to you, and you broke it. From that brokenness, God taught me to open my mouth and speak up for lonely, brokenhearted children in our midst.

I'll never forget you.

Summer In Sweetland

Volume 3 - Never Too Old

also with Kathi Macias and Anne Baxter Campbell

Chapter One

"What's up?" Celia Evers asked breathlessly. She balanced her cell phone on her shoulder while she shut down her computer and grabbed a couple of files to take home in preparation for the next day's court hearings. Glancing at the clock she winced, realizing that it was already almost seven.

"The sky, last I checked," her husband said.

"Homer, you're the king of corny jokes. Seriously, I know I'm running late, but I'm leaving now. I promise I won't be long."

"Yeah, I've heard that before," Homer Evers said. "I was calling to ask if you can pick up Rocky and CJ at the Y. They wanted to stay for the free swim time after their classes, but I had to get home and get dinner going. Sammy's nose is running like a faucet, so I hate to take him out again if I can help it."

"Okay, sure. Did you leave your cell phone with Rocky so I can call them, or do I need to park and go inside?" Celia flicked off the light to her office and bumped the door closed with her hip, striding across the street toward the parking lot the Department of Social Services shared with the county courthouse and jail.

"You'll have to go inside, sorry. I let Dev take the phone. He's doing a school project at the library, and I wanted him to call before he starts walking home. And by the way, when you get home, Jackie wants to talk to you. Says it's important."

Driving toward the YMCA, Celia wondered what her seventeen-year-old daughter wanted to talk about. It must be seriously important, she mused, because getting Jackie to open up had been like pulling teeth. She liked to talk, but not about her feelings—something not uncommon among children who experienced early-life trauma.

Twenty minutes later, Celia turned her car onto Main Street with her moody preteen daughter, Rocky, in the back and her chatty son, CJ, in front. The lingering scent of chlorine emanating from CJ made it clear that once again he forgot to shower after swim class.

"Look, Mom, there's Dev," CJ said, pointing down the street.

He was right. Dev was walking toward home from the library, blissfully unaware of his surroundings, his hands stuffed in his pockets and headphones snuggly clasped onto both ears. Shaking her head, Celia pulled over and stopped at the intersection ahead of Dev, honking her horn. By the third honk, he looked up and trotted over to the car. The fourteen-year-old opened the front door and hooked his thumb toward the back seat, wordlessly pulling rank on his nine-year-old brother.

******

Homer greeted the motley crew at the door, lightly kissing Celia on the forehead while taking the bundle of soggy towels from CJ. He grinned. "Glad to see you found Dev. I feel better now that all my stray sheep are home."

"Speaking of sheep, it smells like shepherd's pie in here. Am I right?"

"The nose knows." Homer chuckled, pointing to the plates on the long oak table in the next room. "Hope you don't mind, but Jackie and I already ate. She has a lot of homework to do before your talk, and I didn't want her eating alone. But I'll sit and chat with you guys while you eat."

"I'm not really hungry, Dad," Dev said, heading down the hall.

"That's okay. You can still sit with us. It's our only family time of the day. How's the project on Code Talkers coming along?"

4

Dev shuffled over to the table while Homer scooped Shepherd's Pie onto the waiting plates. Shaking his head, Dev replied, "I like the project; it's really interesting. Do you know there were some high-ranking Marines who believed the U.S. would never have taken Iwo Jima if not for the Code Talkers?"

"That's pretty cool, Dev. You seem excited about what you're learning. So I don't get why you rolled your eyes and shook your head when Dad asked you about it," Celia said.

"I am excited about it," Dev said. "But I'm also annoyed. Some of the other kids think I picked this topic because it's about Indians and I'm Indian."

Homer burst out laughing.

CJ's eyes bugged out. "Dude, I'm only nine and I know American Indians aren't the same as people from India!" Soon they were all laughing and talking, catching up on their day and enjoying the comfort food.

"Scrape and stack!" Homer reminded the kids while he went to the bottom of the stairwell to call Jackie down. "Jackie, come on down for our evening prayer, then you and Mom can talk while you do dishes."

******

"Dad says you want to talk?" Celia was too impatient to wait for Jackie to begin, so she jumped in while she filled the sink with soapy water.

"Yeah, it's about my friend Wendy? You know, the girl on the track team? The one who's really good at hurdles?" Jackie had a way of making nearly everything that came out of her mouth sound like a question.

"Sure, I remember her. She's really something on those hurdles."

"Well…" Jackie was clearly struggling to find words, so she finished drying three plates before continuing. Then the words tumbled out in a torrent. "Mom, you know how you're a social worker? Well you gotta help. Please? Wendy is super smart and, you know, she wants to go to college, right? But she told me today she's flunking English and gym. Gym! She's a track star, right? Mom, how can she flunk gym? She told me she's flunking on purpose! You know? It doesn't make any sense."

When Jackie paused for air, Celia asked, "You're right, Jackie, it doesn't sound very sensible. Did she say why she's flunking those classes? And what makes you think she needs social work help?"

"Well… Thing is, Mom, she lives at that group home. The one out by the cemetery? She hates it there, Mom. I mean, she tells everyone it's cool, but you know, I guess 'cuz I'm adopted she, like, tells me how she really feels, you know?"

"Oh. I see. Now it's beginning to make sense. I imagine she's scared about what will happen to her once she graduates. She'll have to leave the group home, and if she doesn't have a family she's probably worried she won't have any place to go. So if she flunks a couple of classes, she can stay in high school and the group home one more year before facing an uncertain future. Does that sound about right?"

"Yes, Mom. See? I knew you'd understand. Can you talk to her?" Jackie surprised Celia with a rare hug.

"Maybe we could invite her over for dinner. I can't be her social worker, Jackster; I'm sure she already has one. But we can get to know her a little better, and we can help her form some connections in the community so facing her graduation won't seem so scary."

******

"Here we are," Homer said, turning around to Wendy in the back seat.

"Thanks so much for dinner. And I really appreciate the ride home, Mr. and Mrs. Evers. Do you mind coming in for a minute to meet Roger, the night staff person? I need an adult to sign me in when I'm out after eight o'clock." Wendy Jergens shyly glanced from Homer to Celia.

"Sure, we can come in for a few minutes, Wendy. It was lovely to have you for dinner. I hope you can come again. I'm glad you and Jackie became friends. You have so much in common."

The adults strode toward the side door of the group home as Jackie and Wendy dawdled behind them, clearly not wanting the evening to end. No sooner were they inside than one of the other girls bolted up to Wendy. "Can your friend stay long enough for a couple games of Ping-Pong? Shira isn't here, so we need someone to take her place to play doubles."

Homer nodded when Jackie raised a questioning eyebrow at him. She shed her spring jacket and accepted the proffered Ping-Pong paddle. "I'm Veronica," the tall, gangly girl said. "Who are you?"

"Jackie Evers. I run track with Wendy."

While the girls played, Homer and Celia perched on the edge of the worn sofa, listening to the conversation. When Veronica mentioned she loved animals, Homer asked, "Do you have an after-school job, Veronica? I know they're looking to hire someone at the Beaks and Fins Pet Shop. The owner comes into Deanie's every day for breakfast, complaining that he can't find good help for the afternoon hours."

"That would be a dream job, Mr. Evers, being with animals every day. I'd have to clear it with the staff here and my caseworker, and figure out transportation." Her face beamed. "Do you think your friend would really hire a group-home girl?"

******

In the car on the way home, Celia smiled. Her usually introspective daughter had been opening up so much more lately.

From the back seat, Jackie spoke up. "Thanks, Mom. And Dad, you too. I knew you'd help Wendy, right? I hope you can help her find a family. You know? She could be adopted, right? Like me? I told her that, but she thinks she's too old and no one would want her. She was surprised to hear I was adopted when I was fifteen. And you were super nice to the other girls, too. It made me feel good, you know?"

"Thank you, Jackie, for reaching out to your friend. We're really proud of you. We liked all the girls. It was a fun evening," Celia replied.

Homer nodded. "That's right. I'm hoping we can help Veronica get a job at Beaks and Fins. I had after-school jobs when I was her age; it really made a difference and helped me see possibilities in life I'd never thought about. I think she'll do okay, that Veronica. But her Ping-Pong partner, Misty, she's the one I'm worried about. She seemed so sullen. Depressed even. She hardly said two words. She's definitely going onto my prayer list."

As they pulled into the driveway, Celia pursed her lips. "She might well be depressed. I asked if she had any family in the area and she just said, 'I ain't got nobody.' Such a lonely place to be at such a tender age. Now you have a glimpse of why I work so hard for the kids on my caseload. I don't ever want any of them to say they 'ain't got nobody' when they're about to age out of the system."

Chapter Two

It was a rare treat for Celia to enjoy morning coffee with her husband. Homer stayed home from his breakfast shift at Deanie's Diner so he could go to their son Billy's court hearing. They'd have about fifteen minutes to themselves after the other children left for school, Jackie and Dev on foot to the junior-senior high school and Rocky, CJ, and Sammy by bus to the elementary.

"I'm a little worried about sending Sammy to school today. His cough is worse again," Homer said, stepping back into the house after securing Sammy's wheelchair on the bus.

"I hope he'll be all right, at least until after court. Then you can go bring him home if you have to. Coffee?" Celia asked, not waiting for an answer as she filled his cup. "I wish I could be at Billy's hearing, but I have cases of my own in the other courtroom. I'm so glad Billy drew Judge Stephens. He at least tries to listen to parents and kids before making decisions, unlike Judge Robbins. Robbins aggravates me so much with his 'the apple doesn't fall far from the tree' mentality, always assuming parents either don't care or are bad influences on their kids. Anyway, don't let me start down that road. Let's talk about what we hope will happen at Billy's hearing."

Celia and Homer briefly reviewed the facts. Billy had been arrested with two other boys, including "Little Mike" Carson, son of the Pastor at the Assembly of God church in town, and Terrell Jackson, a youngster being raised by his grandfather, Hal. The boys were accused of setting fire to some outbuildings on the Sweetbriar estate the previous October on Mischief Night, not long after the Williams' house had burned to the ground. They boys confessed to the Sweetbriar fires, calling it a "stupid prank," but they had been adamant they had nothing to do with the Williams' fire.

Yet emotions ran high in town. Even though the boys hadn't been in trouble before, all three were sentenced to a year at Rosebriar County Regional Juvenile Detention Center, generally referred to as "Juvie." Conditions at Juvie were harsh, with the boys frequently reporting untreated injuries, insufficient food, and unchecked bullying. Just before Christmas, Little Mike had been found dead in his room. It was reported as a suicide, but suspicions remained. Pastor Mike didn't believe his son would kill himself. At the review hearing today, the Evers planned to advocate for Billy to be released in time to start the new school year just before Labor Day, instead of serving the full year of his sentence.

Homer filled Celia in on a conversation he'd had yesterday with Pastor Mike and Hal Jackson while they ate breakfast at the diner. They had talked about the worsening conditions at Juvie. Pastor Mike told Homer and Hal about the new support group in town for people with recent losses in their family. The group had met a few times at Arlene Smith's house. Pastor Mike attended, and it had been helping him cope with his grief over Little Mike's death. That gave him the idea of starting a similar group for parents of kids locked up at Juvie. He wanted to know if Hal and Homer would be interested in joining such a group.

"Oh, that sounds like a great idea, Homer. If we band together, maybe we can push for changes at that place. Make it safer and more humane for kids that get sent there. Or shut it down altogether. I can't stand the thought of a place that keeps kids in what basically amounts to cages." Celia shivered, her eyes filling with tears. Homer gently caressed her cheek, and the two were silent for a moment.

"But back to this morning. Do you expect Felix and Officer Livingston to be at the hearing?" Celia asked.

"Juliet tells me her brother plans to come." His co-worker at the diner, Juliet Venetti was a sister to Felix Batista, the fireman who had been first on the scene at both the Sweetbriar fire and the Williams' house fire. "She says Felix doesn't think the kids were involved with the Williams' fire. The fire they started was totally amateurish, while the Williams fire looked more professional, at least to his eye."

"I hope he'll tell the judge that. It might help. You never know. What about Officer Livingston? He's the one who worries me. He's not a very nice man. I've heard he's even been known to kick his mother's dog!"

"Don't go spreading rumors, Silly-Cee. You don't want to get on the bad side of the Livingston family." On that note, both adults set their coffee mugs by the sink and headed for the door.

******

Celia and Homer chatted in hushed tones while waiting to get through security at the Rosebriar County Courthouse. Her phone began to buzz in her pocket. She pushed a button and held it to her ear. "What? You're kidding! Okay, thanks for letting me know." She pressed 'End' and looked woefully at Homer. "Today's courtrooms have been reversed. Judge Stephens will preside over the dependency cases, while Judge Robbins will hear the delinquency cases, including Billy's hearing. I'm so disappointed. He'll never listen to you. He's going to throw the hammer at Billy and Terrell," she said, tears threatening her eyes.

"Don't work yourself up, Cee. We need to trust the outcome to God, not whichever judge is up to bat. Besides, won't having Judge Stephens on the foster care side be better for your cases today?"

"Well, yes, that's true. Still, I felt like Billy had at least a fighting chance before; now I feel..." Her voice trailed off as she saw Officer Randall Livingston stride purposefully down the hall past security. "Oh great, that seals it," she murmured.

******

It had been forty-five minutes since the lunch break and Celia was still waiting for her four cases to be called. Court days were so frustrating. Hurry up and wait, as they say. The door to the waiting room opened and Wendy stepped in with a young woman who must be her caseworker. She shyly waved to Celia and took a seat, pulling a book from her backpack. Celia scooted closer to Wendy and asked her how school was going.

"It's, well, it's okay. I'm having a little trouble with a few classes. But it'll work out."

"I see you're reading *The Epic of Son-Jara*. That's a powerful story."

Wendy's eyes lit up. "Really? You know it? I love ancient stories. I guess that makes me odd, but I see so many parallels with my own life. It's fascinating that a story told so long ago could help me understand my life better than most of the people who know me. I mean, the way Son-Jara had to move around so much after being exiled. It's a lot like life in foster care. I'm thinking of majoring in African studies if I get to go to college, but people tell me I wouldn't be able to use that degree for any real-world jobs." Wendy sighed as the door opened and the court clerk ushered another caseworker with three children into the courtroom.

Wendy wrote a note and passed it to Celia.

Is it true that teenagers like me can be adopted? My caseworker says I'm too old. She wants me to sign up for a supervised independence program and get an apartment, but I'm not so sure I'm ready for that.

Hastily, Celia scribbled on the back of the note and passed it back to Wendy:

Never too old. Tell the judge you want a family. He'll listen.

After Celia's cases were completed, Wendy's case was called. Celia gave the girl a smile she hoped was encouraging and whispered a quick prayer that the judge would listen to this sweet girl's heart and desire for a family. "Please. Lord, I know you want Wendy to have a family of her own, a family for a lifetime. Open doors for her today. Let her see that unlike Son-Jara, she has not been exiled. You have a place and a family for her."

Stepping into the hallway, Celia tried to be discreet as she checked her cell phone for messages from Homer. None. Billy's case must still be underway. She headed for Courtroom Four-B on the fourth floor. Just as she got off the elevator, Celia was surprised to see Homer walking towards her with Pastor Mike, Hal, Felix Batista, and Randall Livingston. All of the men smiled, talking amicably.

"I was hoping I'd catch Billy's case, but looks like I missed it," Celia said to Homer. "How'd it go?"

"Better than we hoped. Judge Robbins wasn't so bad. He agreed it would be in the boys' best interests to start school on time in the fall. He set another review hearing for early August. If progress reports from Rosebriar Juvie are good, he'll release the boys back into the community. Both Terrell and Billy, plus another boy whose case he heard today too."

As they walked toward their car, Celia asked Homer for details, wondering especially about the roles Felix and Officer Livingston played in the outcome. She was shocked to learn that both men testified in ways that proved to be helpful to the boys' cases. Before she could say more, her phone began to buzz. She answered it and heard a girl's voice talking too fast to understand.

"Whoa, slow down. I can't understand you. And I don't recognize this number. Who is this?" Celia would have guessed it was a youth on her caseload. To her surprise, it was Wendy.

"Mrs. Evers, you're the best! I did what you said. After my caseworker recommended to the judge about getting me into the supervised independence program, he asked me what I wanted. I was so shocked I almost couldn't speak, but I had your note in my pocket and it gave me courage. I told the judge that what I really wanted was a family of my own. He asked me if I had any families in mind. The question caught me off guard, but I told him about a few families that had been kind to me in the past, especially the Dawkins family in New Beckton."

"That's great, Wendy. How did you get to know them?"

"Mr. Dawkins was my World Literature teacher when I was in foster care in New Beckton. He's the first teacher who ever got me excited about learning. And I met his wife once at a school open house. She was really nice. I don't really know them, but they seem like such a great family. Do you think I'm crazy?"

"No, I don't think you're crazy at all, Wendy. I think you're brave and strong. I believe you'll get a family of your own. I'm really proud of you for speaking up for yourself today, and I'm so happy to hear that Judge Stephens listened to you."

Celia glowed as she filled Homer in on the events of her day and the outcome of Wendy's hearing. They drove home filled with gratitude that today was not just one more day of tilting at the twin windmills of the foster care and juvenile justice systems, but also a day flecked with surprising glimmers of hope.

"I can't wait to tell Jackie about Wendy speaking up for herself," Celia mused. "I'm proud of our girl for being an advocate for her friend. She seems so icy-cold at times, but moments like these prove she has a golden heart."

"I agree." Homer grasped Celia's hand, giving it a squeeze. "Oh, on another note, did you remember that I promised to bring a tray of fajitas to Rocky's class tomorrow as part of their Heritage Day celebration? Do we have the ingredients, or should we stop on the way home?"

Chapter Three

Celia wiggled her toes and stretched her arms over her head while looking at the clock. Seven forty-five. What a treat not to have to rush off anywhere this Saturday morning! Next to her, Homer slept, so she slipped out of bed quietly. The whole house was still, and the sky outside was already painted pale blue. After making a steaming cup of coffee, Celia shrugged into an old cardigan, picked up her Bible, and walked out to the front porch for a little quiet time before the day began.

Opening her Bible, Celia removed the small envelope filled with photos and began her morning tradition of praying for people she loved while looking at their pictures. She worked her way from youngest to oldest. She thanked God for Sammy's cheerful disposition and asked that he would gain physical strength. It had been a long winter for him with one cold or flu on top of another. CJ's goofy picture brought a smile to her face, and she remembered to pray that God would help him focus more, especially in school.

"Rocky, Rocky, Rocky, what are we going to do about you?" Celia murmured to herself, fingering the unsmiling photo of their striking but sullen Mexican-American daughter, Lydia Rochelle— a.k.a. Rocky. She hadn't quite finished her litany of morning conversations with God when Homer stepped onto the porch, coffee in hand, to join her. After praying together, they began to outline their plans for the day, plans that included a trip to Juvie at 1:45 for their weekly thirty-minute visit with Billy. Remembering he needed more socks and had also requested a notebook and pen, they agreed to allow time for a stop at the dollar store uptown.

Hearing the shower, Celia stood up. "I think I'll make breakfast quiches."

Homer responded by noisily smacking his lips.

"Goofball," she chuckled, striding toward the kitchen.

An hour later the enticing smells of bacon and gooey melting cheese had drawn the entire family to the table. Dev asked for a ride to the library so he could return some books. CJ spilt his orange juice, and Jackie reminded her parents that she couldn't babysit while they went to Juvie because she had track practice that day. With the mention of track, Celia asked Jackie if there were any updates on Wendy or the other girls from the Youth Acres Group Home.

"Wendy's caseworker got in contact with that family in New Beckton. You know, the teacher? Wendy visited them last week, and today they're coming to watch the practice. After that she's going to their house. For the weekend, right? She says she really likes them, but she's kind of scared, too. She's afraid they won't like her when they really get to know her, you know?" Jackie licked the remains of the melted cheese from her fingers. "Veronica got the job at the Beaks and Fins pet store. She's going to work after school and on Saturdays. But Misty still has nobody, Mom." Jackie's shoulders slumped.

After breakfast the Evers plunged into their weekend chores. They stopped at noon to get ready for their trip to the dollar store and Juvie. Jan Symond, their neighbor, came to sit with Sammy. All the other kids left for their Saturday activities.

******

Homer glanced at his watch as they left the dollar store. "We have a little extra time before we can see Billy. Beaks and Fins is right on this block."

He and Celia strolled into the pet store to say hello to Veronica. "She sure seems to enjoy the work, doesn't she?" he murmured to Celia as they watched Veronica feed and tussle with two energetic puppies before securing their cages and turning toward the front of the store.

She beamed as she saw the Evers, bouncing over to greet them. "Guess what? This week we sold a puppy to a really nice lady. She came in every day to look at him, and this morning she bought him and took him home. If I ever was going to have a mom, she's the kind of mom I'd want!"

Homer congratulated Veronica on her new job and nudged Celia toward the door. They needed to leave for Juvie. If they were late they'd miss their visit and have to wait another week to see Billy. Driving east on Main Street, Homer did a double-take as they passed the offices of Livingston Investigations. "Isn't that the other girl we met at the group home? The quiet one. What was her name? Misty?"

"You're right. It *is* her. I wonder why she'd be going into a private eye's office. Whatever it is, she looks determined but not exactly happy. Come to think of it, I don't think I've ever seen her smile," Celia said.

******

An hour later, Celia was the one not smiling. Their visit with Billy had come and gone, and it would be another week before they could see him again, with just one phone call allowed in between.

Hal Jackson walked out of Juvie with the Evers, his eyes rimmed with tears. "You know, it's kind of my fault Terrell wound up here. If I'd been stricter about who she hung around with, his mother wouldn't have gotten hooked on drugs. I wanted to make it up to the boy and paid a lot more attention to him. I feel like such a failure with both of them."

Homer shook his head. "No, Hal, none of this is your fault. Although trust me, I do understand feeling guilty. Celia and I go there sometimes too. You've got to trust that you've done the best you could and have faith that God's grace is still sufficient. And now we all can use our experiences to help others, you know."

Hal shrugged and nodded.

******

Celia got into the car, watching as Homer lingered with Hal for a few extra minutes. Homer made a call on his cell phone before opening the door and getting into the driver's seat. He told her he'd set a date for Hal and Pastor Mike to have breakfast with him at the diner to work on plans for a parent support group. "We're going to ask Felix Batista and Randall Livingston to join us for the meeting too. We got this crazy idea that they might make great mentors for some of the boys here at Juvie. What do you think, Cee?"

"Felix, sure, but Officer Livingston?" Celia shook her head and laughed. Before Billy's court hearing she'd thought of Randall Livingston as an enemy. But who knows? Maybe he could become a friend and mentor to one of the boys at Juvie. Not all of the teens had family visiting them. Some of the boys' families were hours away and not able to make the weekly trip.

To some people this was just more evidence that the families didn't care, but Celia knew better. She'd seen the pain of parents who felt shut out of their children's lives, both in the foster care and the juvenile justice system. It was heart-wrenching. Turning these thoughts over in her mind, she turned to Homer. "Well, Officer Livingston does only work part time, so he might be available. It's not a bad idea, Homer Evers—not bad at all."

******

Homer dropped Celia off at home to relieve Jan Symonds and check on Sammy, then he headed out to collect the other kids from their respective activities. He spent a few minutes watching the end of track practice before the sweaty Jackie flopped into the car. Homer reminded Jackie she would be in charge tonight while he and Celia had their weekly "date night," dinner at Gentry's and a movie.

******

By 6:15, the kids had been fed and settled in for the evening, Jackie armed for babysitting with the newest acquisitions from Netflix. Homer and Celia drove toward Gentry's restaurant. "Isn't that Misty?" Celia asked, pointing at the girl trudging along the side of the road.

Homer pulled the car up next to Misty. "Would you like a ride?"

Misty threw them a suspicious look. "I guess. Can you give me a ride to Gentry's?"

"We saw you over by Livingston Investigations earlier today, and now Gentry's restaurant. That's quite an interesting way for a teen to spend a Saturday," Homer said, hoping the girl would open up. She glared at him and said nothing for a moment.

With a resigned sigh she said, "I went to Livingston's to see if I could hire them to find my family. I haven't heard anything from or about them since I came into foster care nearly twelve years ago. I've been in foster homes in four different towns, but I was once told my great-grandparents used to live on a farm by Sweetland, close to the river."

"No kidding?" Home said. "That's pretty neat."

"I've heard I'm biracial, but I'm not even sure about that. I thought private investigators would help me, but they turned me down because they don't accept minors as clients. However, they told me about the 'town historian,' Rozene Gentry, and they called her to say I wanted to talk to her. So," Misty concluded, "I'm going to Gentry's to meet this Rozene lady because she told Chelsea at the detective place she'd help me."

"Good luck, Misty," Celia said as they pulled up to the restaurant. "Would you like a ride back to Youth Acres after we have dinner? If you're still here, anyway."

When Misty nodded and went into the restaurant ahead of them to find Rozene, Celia winked and grinned at Homer. "There aren't any good movies playing this weekend, anyway."

Like Celia, Homer sympathized deeply with this lost girl. "No child should have to work so hard just to find someone to belong to."

Chapter Four

I need this recipe, Celia Evers thought as she finished off the last bite of the tasty corn muffin that comprised her lunch. The muffin had been left over from last night's inaugural meeting of the "Sweetland Families for Justice" at Hal Jackson's home. Eight adults had attended, including Pastor Mike, Hal, Felix Batista, Randall Livingston, and two other parents of teens currently in Juvie , along with Homer and Celia.

The group agreed to support one another and to advocate for the changes needed at Juvie to improve safety and create opportunities for the children sent there. Maybe the most important goal had been to develop a mentoring program to foster more community involvement with the teens and their families. Surprisingly, Officer Livingston had agreed to head up that effort.

A moment later, the light on her phone blinked. When Celia picked up the receiver, Angie, the DSS administrative assistant, told her she had a call from Anne Goodman, a nurse at the Sweetland Hospital. Celia felt her heart sink. A call from the hospital often meant a newly abused child had been admitted and needed a social work assessment.

Steeling herself to hear painful details about a broken child, Celia was surprised when Nurse Goodman said she was calling about Misty Keys, the hard-to-reach teen from the Youth Acres Group home where both Wendy and Veronica lived.

"I know you aren't Misty's caseworker. She's actually on her way from Harrellsonville," Anne began. "But when we asked Misty who we could call on her behalf, she kept repeating that she had 'nobody.' After talking to her a little longer, she finally blurted out your name. Actually she mentioned both you and your husband. She said you'd been kind to her a few weeks ago and you'd helped some of the other girls in the group home. So I decided to take a chance and call you."

"Why is she in the hospital? Is she hurt?"

"I'm afraid Misty tried to kill herself last night by cutting her wrists with jagged glass from a broken mirror. She didn't succeed, and she was angry that her efforts to end her life were intercepted." The nurse paused, as Celia choked back tears. "I've gotten a little more involved in this case than I usually do. I have a twenty-year-old daughter, and I keep thinking how grateful I am she's never faced this level of depression. How can a child so young and full of promise with a whole future ahead of her want to end her life? I just don't understand."

"I know how you feel, Anne," Celia said, swiping at her now wet cheeks. "So many of the children in foster care feel especially vulnerable as they get close to their eighteenth birthdays if they have no family or close network of support. The thought of aging out of the system and being totally alone in the world can be overwhelming. The future doesn't look so promising from that vantage point."

"I never thought of it that way," Anne said. "I recently met another girl from the group home. Her name is Veronica. One of the animals from the pet shop needed veterinary care, and Veronica was charged with bringing the sick puppy to Dr. Finders' office. I'd also been at the vet's office that day with my fifteen-year-old son, Tim, while he completed his application for a summer job with Dr. Finders. That young lady seemed so bubbly, full of life. Tim and Dr. Finders invited her to come to our youth group at the Community Church. I got such a positive feeling about the girls from the group home just by meeting that one girl. I never thought about all the turmoil they've been through."

Celia nodded. "I'm so glad you met Veronica. She's a lovely young girl. Connecting her with Dr. Finders is perfect. I'd forgotten he leads the youth group. That should be a great connection for her. Each youth in foster care is different, but maybe some of them would be willing to visit Misty while she's in the hospital. Homer, Jackie, and I could stop by on Saturday after we visit with Billy." Celia ended the call and glanced at her watch. Oops, she was now late for a staff meeting. Gathering her files and blinking back the remainder of her tears, she hustled down the hall, hoping she hadn't been missed yet.

******

After a full morning of sprucing up the yard in preparation for their annual Memorial Day picnic, Celia and Homer freshened up and drove to Juvie for their weekly visit with Billy. He'd had a tough week, and their last phone call was depressing. She hoped he'd feel more upbeat today. He seemed to love seeing her and Homer each week, but he really missed his siblings and school friends. Celia gathered a stack of recent pictures to share with him in hopes of lifting his spirits. After they picked up Jackie and Wendy up from their track practice, they could all visit Misty at the hospital. They arrived at Juvie seconds after Hal pulled in, and the three friends chatted comfortably on their way to sign in at the visitors' desk. Celia, Homer, and Hal all showed their IDs. The guard told Hal to wait a few minutes, but Celia and Homer were ushered into the parents' lounge.

"Are you up for our weekly chess game, Son?" Homer asked as he pulled his portable chess set out of his backpack. The two set up the pieces and began to play.

Billy seemed happy to see them, although Celia couldn't help but notice the dark circles under his eyes. She knew he hadn't been sleeping well, and he looked so thin. *I can't wait to get him out of here*, she thought, glancing around the room at all the other parents and grandparents playing out this same ritual with their teenage children and grandchildren.

Throughout their thirty-minute visit with Billy, Celia was aware that Hal and Terrell had not entered the room. Although the cold visiting room with its plastic tables and wooden benches was crowded, she was certain she'd have noticed Hal and especially Terrell because he was so tall. She tried to dismiss the foreboding feeling of trouble and focused her attention on Billy. Too quickly their time was over and they gave Billy bear-hugs before the guard herded the teens back to their quarters.

Stepping out into the hot May air that caused local residents to call their town "Sweatland," Celia heard the sound of muffled sobbing coming from the direction of their car. She rounded the corner of the building and gaped at Hal Jackson hunched over his steering wheel.

******

Homer got to him first. "Hal! Hal, what is it? Is it Terrell? Has something happened?" Memories of Little Mike's death the previous December surfaced in Homer's mind, and he held his breath as he waited to hear what Hal might say.

Hal scrubbed at his eyes. "They wouldn't let me see Terrell. All they would say was that Terrell is in solitary confinement 'for his own good.' They wouldn't give me any further explanation."

Homer grimaced. Being in locked detention facilities could be corrosive to the spirits of developing teens, but time spent in solitary confinement would be ten times more traumatic, eating away at their very souls.

The "Sweetland Families for Justice" group had begun research on the impact of detention on youth. They wanted to learn about better, more humane, and more effective ways to support positive development, while at the same time correcting delinquent behaviors to keep the community safe. This new crisis was likely to jolt their newly formed little group into higher gear.

After promising to call Hal later in the evening, Homer and Celia set out to pick up Jackie and Wendy. "Boy, nothing like going from the frying pan to the fire today. It's painful to see so many of Sweetland's young people struggling so much, and to see the impact it has on their family and friends is almost too much to bear." Homer guided the car into a parking spot near the high school soccer field. "I really hate that Jackie and Wendy have to see their friend in a psych unit."

"Better than seeing her in the morgue," Celia said. "At least they have each other. I hope Misty will realize that in spite of not having a family, she's not entirely alone."

******

After checking in at the front desk, the little band of visitors made their way to the third floor. Two women came out of Misty's room just as the new arrivals prepared to enter. Anne Goodman introduced herself and her daughter Kimberly to Celia and her crew, explaining that she used a little of her "off" time to visit Misty because she simply couldn't get the girl out of her mind and heart.

Misty stared at a teddy bear holding a bouquet of balloons as they entered her room. Upon seeing Wendy and Jackie, Misty's eyes filled. "I'm so sorry. I'm so sorry that I'm such a loser. I fail at everything. I even failed at killing myself. How pathetic is that?"

Jackie and Wendy rushed to her bedside and smothered her with hugs.

"You're not a loser, Misty. And you're not alone. I need you," Wendy said. "Veronica, Shira, Melanie—we all need you. None of us at the group home have families, so we have to be a family for each other. You can't leave us; you just can't." Softly, Wendy began to cry.

Jackie remained quiet, her eyes bearing witness that she was revisiting her own world of grief for a moment.

"You're about to have a family, Wendy," Misty said, "That Dawkins family, they're going to adopt you, and then you'll be gone just like the others. Everyone gets a family and leaves. That's just the way it works. Everyone but me. I ain't got nobody, and I just gotta get over it. Besides, I'm practically an adult. I don't know why I was so interested in finding a family anyway. Who needs a family? I can handle my own life just fine."

"I'm not sure, Misty," Wendy said. "I don't know if I'm going to let them adopt me. I don't think I'm ready. And I know they won't still want me when they know me better. But even if they do—well, what I'm saying is, you'll always be my sister. Nothing will change that, Misty. I love you, girl."

By this time, all three girls were crying, while Celia barely contained her own tears. She glanced up at Homer and saw the moisture filling his eyes too.

Suddenly, Jackie found her voice. "Y'all cut it out now. You know? You have to have faith. Two years ago, I didn't think anyone would ever want me. I was in a group home too, up in Harrellsonville. My life looked hopeless. But look at me, right? Look! I got adopted. I thought I was too old. You know? But I learned you're never too old. I know you're both going to get your own family too. And I'm not going to stop praying until it comes true!"

Making eye contact with Homer in that moment was a mistake, and Celia knew it instantly. As soon as she caught his eye, she couldn't hold the tears back for another second.

Chapter Five

There was a festive mood in the air as the entire town of Sweetland gathered for the final track meet of the season against their archrivals from New Beckton High. Walking towards the bleacher seats, pushing Sammy in his wheelchair and keeping an eye on CJ as he scampered ahead, Homer nudged Celia. "Look. There are Carl and Lorraine Dawkins coming our way."

He raised his voice. "So, cheering for Sweetland or New Beckton today, folks?" Homer grinned, knowing Carl was a teacher at New Beckton High.

"It's a no-brainer, Homer. I love my job, but I love my family more. And Wendy's family now, even though it won't be official for a couple more months. So we're on your side of the stands today, my friend." They walked with the Evers to the bleacher section with the wheelchair ramp, filling them in on the plans to finalize their adoption of Wendy before her eighteenth birthday, which fell a few days after Labor Day.

"She's tested us; for a while she said no, no, no every time we talked about adoption. But that all changed after her friend Misty was in the hospital," Lorraine said. "On another note, I brought you some strawberries from the patch in our yard. Wendy says Jackie's been asking for them. Something about a special family recipe?"

Celia laughed. "Yes, Nanna's Strawberry Squares. She's been begging me to make a batch now that the berries are fresh. We were planning to serve it for the graduation party next week. We hope your family will stop over."

"Wouldn't miss it."

"Great. Their friend Veronica is coming too. She hasn't connected with a family yet, but we still have hope. In the meantime, she's loving that job at Beaks and Fins, and they love her there too."

"Families come in lots of different shapes and sizes. Maybe she'll find hers through the pet shop," Lorraine said.

Before they could continue the conversation, a group of four men clambered up and sat on the bleacher seats in front of the Evers and Dawkins. "Well, if it isn't half of the "Sweetland Families for Justice" committee," Homer laughed. "I think we might have a quorum! What are you all being so noisy about?"

Hal grinned. "Pastor Mike, Randall, and Felix are all going with me to Juvie for visiting time after the track meet today to support me in making sure I can see Terrell. We're having a meeting next week before everyone is too caught up in summer plans. We need to finalize our strategy for bringing the juvenile justice reform recommendations to the Governor and state legislature when they reconvene just after Labor Day." Without missing a beat, Hal pulled a stapled packet of papers from his satchel and handed it to the Dawkins, inviting them to join the cause.

After reading the *Juvenile Justice Family Bill of Rights* that had been handed to her, Lorraine said, "I'm really impressed with this. The whole time we've been visiting with Wendy and preparing to adopt her, God has given us a heart for the other girls at the group home. Especially girls like Misty who have no family. No one to visit on holidays or give them guidance as they navigate into the adult world. We're thinking of starting a group at our church to support and advocate for these girls. Your work here has inspired me to stop thinking and start doing something. It's time for action."

At that moment, the starting gun boomed and the adults were on their feet, cheering Wendy on. As she glided effortlessly from one jump to the next, Celia shouted, "You go girl! No hurdle's too high for you!"

Summer in Sweetland

Volume Three "Never Too Old"

Recipes

Homer's Shepherd's Pie

Ingredients

2 lbs. ground beef or similar quantity of veggie crumbles
1 onion
1 clove of garlic
Optional: ½ each of a green and a red pepper
Optional: 6 large mushrooms
Cooking spray or 1 tsp. cooking oil
5 lbs. potatoes
½ stick of butter
½ cup of milk or cream
Optional: butter and cream can be replaced with veggie broth
3 cups frozen corn
Salt and pepper to taste,
Optional: ½ cup shredded cheddar or Parmesan cheese
Catsup and sour cream for serving

Directions

1. Quarter potatoes and bring to a boil in salted water. Boil 20 minutes or until fork-tender.
2. Dice the onion and finely chop the garlicIf using the peppers and mushrooms, dice these as well.
3. In a skillet heat the cooking spray or oil and add the diced onion, garlic, peppers and mushrooms. Sauté until onions are golden.
4. Add ground beef or veggie crumbles and cook until browned. Drain most of the grease and set the meat/veggie crumbles aside.
5. Defrost the corn.
6. When potatoes are finished, drain water and add butter, cream (or broth), along with salt and pepper. Mash until you are happy with the consistency, adding more liquid if needed.
7. Make a layer of the ground beef/onion mixture on the bottom of a casserole-style pan, then add a layer of corn, top with the mashed potatoes.
8. Bake at 400 degrees for 20 minutes.
9. If using the cheese option, add cheese and broil for a final minute to melt the cheese.

10.   Serve with catsup and sour cream.

CJ's Fajitas for a Crowd

Ingredients:

1 3-4 pound whole chicken
Oregano
2 cloves of Garlic, crushed
Cayenne pepper
Cinnamon
Salt
2 tbsp. Olive oil
Juice from 2 limes
3 tbsp. Olive Oil
2 each red, yellow and green bell peppers, julienned
2 medium yellow onions, thinly sliced
1 clove garlic, diced
Cayenne pepper
Your favorite hot sauce
2 15.5-ounce cans black beans, rinsed
1 16-ounce package frozen corn
1 or 2 4-ounce cans (depending on your taste) diced green chilies
2 16 ounce cans petite diced tomatoes, drained *or* equivalent amount of diced fresh tomatoes
Dash of cinnamon
1 tsp. shavings of unsweetened baking chocolate or baking cocoa
Salt
Pepper
1-2 cups reserved broth from chicken, and up to ¼ cup vegetable broth
Optional: veggie chicken strips
24 fajita-size flour tortillas
3 cups shredded cheese–can be a combination of sharp and mild cheddar, Monterey Jack, and Colby
Optional Ingredient/Garnishes:
2-3 fresh jalapeno peppers, finely diced
Fresh cilantro
Sour cream

Your favorite brand of picante salsa

Directions

1. Place whole chicken in a pot, cover with water, and bring to a boil. Add crushed garlic, 1 tsp. each of oregano, cayenne pepper, salt, and a dash of cinnamon. Adjust amount of seasonings to taste. Boil for 75-90 minutes until meat is falling off the bones. Set aside to cool.
2. Drain chicken, reserving the broth. Bone and skin the chicken, discarding the bones and skin and shredding the chicken meat.
3. In a bowl, whisk together the 2 tbsp. olive oil and the lime juice. Add the shredded chicken and toss to coat. Set aside.
4. In a large frying pan or wok, heat the 3 tbsp. olive oil
5. Add red bell pepper, onions, and garlic; sauté until onions are golden and slightly transparent
6. Add 2 tsp. of cayenne pepper and/or hot sauce (or both). Adjust quantity depending on how much heat you like in your fajitas. Stir well.
7. Add black beans, corn, green chilies, and tomatoes; stir well.
8. Add cinnamon, chocolate, salt, and pepper to taste.
9. Remove approximately 1/6th of the total mixture and put into a smaller frying pan. Set aside.
10.   To the remaining 5/6th in the frying pan or wok, add the marinated chicken and 1 cup of the reserved broth. Heat gently, adding additional broth if needed to thoroughly moisten, but you do not want it to be soupy.
11.   Heat the reserved 1/6th of the vegetable mixture with veggie chicken strips (if using) and a small amount of vegetable broth.

Serving:

1. Warm the tortillas and place in a basket or tortilla-warmer.
2. Create a buffet style line with the tortillas first, followed by the chicken and vegetable mixture, then the vegetarian version of the vegetable mixture. Be sure the meat and veggie versions are clearly labeled. Next comes the bowl of shredded cheese and finally the garnishes.

3. Add a fresh salad and a pitcher of limeade, and you have a complete meal for a crowd!

Celia's Breakfast Quiche

Note: *Celia is a busy working mom with 6 children, including some with special needs. Therefore, her favorite cooking shortcut is to use premade deep-dish frozen piecrusts for her breakfast quiches. She always keeps some in the freezer. However, if you wish to make your own piecrust, the recipe below is a good one for filling with quiche. Also note, Celia usually doubles or triples this recipe for her family, making some with bacon and others with vegetables or plain cheese. This is also her signature dish for potluck gatherings.*

Crust (if not using frozen)

2 cups all purpose flour
½ tsp. salt
½ tsp. sugar
½ cup plus 3   tbsp. shortening (can be margarine, lard, Crisco, or a combination)
5   tbsp. cold water

1. Preheat oven to 400 degrees.
2. Cut the shortening into small pieces (about the size of chocolate chips).
3. Mix the flour, salt, and sugar.
4. Cut the shortening into the flour mixture.
5. Add water and mix well.
6. Divide dough in half, roll each half out and fit into one pie pan.
7. Prick the bottom with a fork, place a layer of dry kidney beans on the bottom, and bake at 400 for 8-10 minutes until done.

Filling

6 eggs
4 cups of milk or cream---best if you use a combination of milk and light cream or half and half
Salt, pepper, paprika, nutmeg, basil

2 cups shredded cheese: Celia's signature is to use a combination of three or more kinds of cheeses. Her favorites include: Swiss, Gruyere, sharp cheddar, mozzarella, and Muenster

1 package bacon

Optional: a package frozen chopped spinach (defrosted with water squeezed out), 1 cup finely chopped broccoli, 1 cup sautéed peppers, onions and/or mushrooms, 1 cup shredded crab meat or cooked baby shrimp

Directions

1. Prepare crusts. If using frozen, defrost and pre-bake according to package directions. After crusts are prepared lower oven temperature to 375 degrees.

2. In a large skillet, cook bacon until crisp, drain grease, and set aside to cool.

3. In a large bowl whisk together the eggs, milk/cream, and approximately 1 tsp. each of salt, pepper, paprika, nutmeg, and basil. Quantities of seasonings may be varied according to taste.

4. In a separate bowl, mix a variety of shredded cheeses.

5. Crumble bacon into the bottom of one precooked piecrust.

6. Select a vegetable or vegetable combination for the second quiche from the options listed. Layer approximately 1 cup of prepared veggies into the bottom of the second crust, OR you may choose to make a second quiche plain cheese. For special occasions, layer a cup of shredded crabmeat or baby shrimp into second piecrust.

7. Layer one cup of cheese on top of bacon and/or veggies (or crab meat or shrimp). If making one quiche plain cheese you may wish to add a little extra cheese.

8. Pour approximately half of the egg/milk mixture into each piecrust. Be careful not to overflow crust. If you have extra egg/milk mixture you can bake separately in a custard cup.

9. Make an aluminum foil collar around the edges of each piecrust, but do not cover the entire pie with foil.

10.   Bake 40 to50 minutes until set. Allow to cool slightly before serving.

Hal's Corn Muffins with Honey Butter

Honey Butter

Cream together 2 sticks unsalted butter, ¼ cup honey, 1 tsp. cayenne pepper and ½ tsp. salt until thoroughly blended. Place in a pottery crock and set aside.

Muffin Ingredients:

2   tbsp. olive oil
½ onion, finely diced
1 clove garlic, finely minced
2 jalapeno peppers, minced, or 1 small can green chilies, drained, or a combination. May also use poblano chilies.
½ cup creamed corn
1 cup flour
1 cup yellow cornmeal
2 tsp. baking powder
1 tsp. baking soda
1 tsp. salt
2 tsp. sugar
6   tbsp. unsalted butter
1 cup buttermilk
3 eggs
1 cup shredded sharp jalapeno cheddar or pepper jack cheese (or mixture of both)

Directions

1. Pre-heat oven to 400 degrees and line muffin tins with paper liners or spray with cooking spray.
2. Sauté onions, peppers, and garlic in olive oil until onions are golden. Add creamed corn and set aside.
3. Mix all dry ingredients in one large bowl.
4. Melt the butter, cool and then mix butter and all wet ingredients in separate bowl
5. Combine dry and wet ingredients
6. Fold in sautéed onion, pepper, and corn mixture
7. Fold in shredded cheese
8. Scoop into prepared muffin tins – makes 12 large or 18 medium muffins
9. Bake for 10 to 12 minutes at 400 degrees
10. Serve with honey butter

Nanna's Strawberry Squares

Ingredients

1¼ cup all-purpose flour
2/3 cup brown sugar
1/3 cup walnuts finely chopped
1/3 cup pecans finely chopped
2/3 cup melted butter
¼ cup semi-sweet mini chocolate chips

2 cups fresh strawberries
1½ cups sugar
3 egg whites
2 tbsp. lemon juice
1 cup heavy (whipping) cream
2 tbsp. chocolate syrup or fudge sauce

½ cup heavy (whipping) cream
2 tsp. sugar
1 tsp. vanilla extract

8 small strawberries, halved
Sprigs of mint

Directions

1. Preheat oven to 350 degrees.
2. Coat a cookie sheet and a 9 x 13 brownie pan with cooking spray.
3. Combine flour, brown sugar, nuts, and melted butter.
4. Spread nut mixture on prepared cookie sheet.
5. Toast in oven for 12 to 15 minutes.
6. Remove from oven and set aside to cool.
7. When nut mixture has cooled, mix in mini-chocolate chips.
8. Press 2/3 of nut mixture into prepared brownie pan.
9. Chop strawberries and coat with the 1½ cups sugar, set aside.
10.   Whip egg whites until soft peaks begin to form, add lemon juice, and continue to whip another minute.

11.   Fold strawberry/sugar mixture into egg whites.

12.   In a separate bowl, whip the 1 cup of heavy whipping cream. Fold into strawberry/egg white mixture.

13.   Pour this mixture on top of nut mixture in brownie pan and smooth top with a spatula.

14.   Freeze for about 30 minutes until semi-set. Then sprinkle the remaining nut mixture on top and drizzle with chocolate syrup.

15.   Freeze for several hours until firm.

16.   Whip remaining heavy cream with sugar and vanilla extract.

To Serve

1. Cut into 16 squares.
2. Add a dollop of whipped cream to each square.
3. Garnish each serving with half of a strawberry and a sprig of mint.

Are We There Yet? The Ultimate Road Trip Adopting & Raising 22 Kids

also with Hector Badeau

This excerpt includes the Foreword along with Chapters 9 & 10

Foreword

We have 22 children, 20 through adoption. Some say that makes us crazy, while others say it makes us saints. To us, it simply makes us sojourners along the path God has set before us, albeit in a somewhat larger caravan than most.

It has been a scary, challenging, thrilling, joyous, confusing, frustrating, and rewarding journey from the day we joined our lives together with vows to travel as a team for the rest of our lives, until today. It has been a journey that we would definitely repeat if we had the opportunity to live our lives over again (with a few course corrections we can now see clearly in hindsight)! So we have written this book, both as a "travelogue" of our personal journey and a bit of a road map for you to consider as you take your own journey—whether your journey includes adoption, parenting, or other adventures.

Hector and I have worked on this book together. It is our story, shared through our eyes and our memories. Through it, we also share many of our children's stories—at least the parts of their stories that are intertwined with our own. We recognize, honor, and value the fact that the fullness of each of their stories belongs only to them, so we have tried to strike a balance between sharing our stories and respecting their privacy.

We decided to write the book in present tense in hopes that as you read, you will feel as though you are traveling alongside of us. We wanted you to experience our stories as they unfolded with both freshness and in anticipation of what will happen next. To accomplish this, most of the book is written in Sue's voice. Yet we wanted to incorporate Hector's voice in a meaningful way, and so we have chosen to include his personal introduction and three standalone chapters—"From a Father's Heart"—throughout the book. These chapters are presented in Hector's voice.

After the introductions, the story begins on our wedding day in 1979 and follows our travels through early 2013. If you wish to know a little more about our own backgrounds, how our childhood experiences shaped our faith and our life vision, and how we met and dated as teenagers, we have included a section in the Afterward on our early years.

Thank you for deciding to take this journey with us. It is our hope that as you read, you can pretend you are sitting in a travel agent's office, and we are your customer service representatives, eager to inspire and tempt you as you plan your own unforgettable trip to all of the magical destinations God has in store for you.

Chapter Nine
David, Trish, Renee

"Sue, you awake?" I can't sleep. Hector whispers to me on our third night back home in our own bed after traveling to Florida for this year's NACAC conference. It was our second year as the official booksellers and we're still worn out from the trip.

"I'm awake, but barely. What's up? It's after 11 and I have to be in the office early in the morning, remember? I'm meeting with the Kirpans about the siblings they're hoping to adopt from Texas."

"I'm glad they are moving forward with that," he says, then continues. "Those six siblings from New Mexico—I just can't get them out of my mind, and I can't sleep. Ever since that social worker told us that they are scattered all over in different homes, I just keep thinking that maybe we can pull them back together as a family."

"I'll call their worker tomorrow and see if I can learn more about what's going on with them," I promise. "But for now, please, let's go to sleep."

"All right. All right."

******

After Todd's adoption last summer, we traveled to NACAC in Toronto with all ten kids, plus our exchange student, Claudia, and ran the official book table for the conference. Following that, the next twelve months flew by in a blur; everything seemed to happen at once. We met the Debolts in person and they invited Rootwings to join their AASK America Network. They came to Vermont and did a fundraiser for us and we raised enough money to hire a director and open an office. I wrote a curriculum called "The Adoption Roadmap" to prepare prospective parents, and we placed our first several children into adoptive homes. It's been a heady, exhilarating time, knowing that we are really helping kids get the one thing they need more than anything—a permanent, loving home.

On weekends Hector and I took turns traveling around the country in our big van, toting boxes of books to sell at conferences and spending one-on-one time with each of the children in turn. We got so busy with the book sales; we hired our friend Doug Farnham to help. Our van broke down more times than we can count, but other than that, life is good.

******

When it was time to attend this year's NACAC conference in Orlando, Florida, we traveled in a caravan, with several other Rootwings families, including the Kirpans from Moretown. As soon as they got involved with Rootwings, Patty and Gary became our closest friends and strongest supporters. Like us, they have a particular heart for sibling groups; they've already adopted four children and are now considering three more.

While at NACAC in Orlando, a social worker from New Mexico stopped by our table to buy some books and recognized us, asking if we were the family that had adopted Abel, SueAnn, George, and Flory. As we continued talking, we asked her if a family had ever been found for the six teens who had been on our hearts for nearly two years. Sadly, we learned that not only were they still waiting for a family, but that they were scattered in different homes across the state of New Mexico.

******

"Look what came in the mail today," Hector says, a week later. "The new *Los Ninos* from New Mexico. But look at this: instead of picturing all six of the kids, they left out the two oldest boys—this time they only have pictures of Lilly, Renee, Trish, and David. I can't believe that. Have you heard anything at all back from the social worker?"

"As a matter of fact, I got a call from her today," I reply. "She told me that they decided to stop looking for a family for JD and Fisher due to their ages, and actually, even though they pictured Lilly in *Los Ninos,* they've decided that they're really only going to focus on the three youngest ones. After two years of looking, they've decided that there just aren't any families for six teenagers."

"That breaks my heart," Hector says. "I know it's hard to find families for all six, but the thought of splitting them up is terrible. Sometimes when things are tough in your family, your siblings are the only people you can trust."

I know Hector knows this, in part, from his own family experience with an alcoholic father. If it weren't for his brother Bernie and his sister Irene, his life might have been very different.

"Two years ago, they weren't interested in our family—we were too young, too white, and lived too far away for them to even look at our home study. I wonder what they'll say now?"

"I asked her to send us the updated information and she said she would. She also asked us to send our most recent home study over to her so she can review it with her supervisor."

"Sounds like a plan for now. In the meantime, let's pray about it. Who knows? We handled six teenage boys at a time at the group home; maybe that was meant to be our training ground. Meanwhile, maybe we should try learning a little sign language," Hector adds, remembering that the youngest of the six siblings, David, is deaf.

******

School begins and, after a few adjustments, we've found our rhythm with ten kids. Hector gets up at five to have his quiet time before the craziness begins. By 7:30 five kids are on the bus to Cabot Elementary School, and George is on his way to school in Barre. Isaac, Raj, Joelle and Todd keep Hector busy at home. His days are filled with mountains of laundry, some house cleaning, and lots of time reading stories—all of our kids love story time! Most days, I head in to Rootwings and work alongside Peter, our executive director, or travel around the state teaching classes to prospective adoptive families.

Occasionally, there is a day like today, when Hector has a Father Grublet project and I stay home with the four little ones. We've just finished snack time and are waiting for the school buses to come up the hill with the big kids when the phone rings.

"Head lice!" I recoil in shock. "I don't understand. How did this happen?" The school nurse in Barre just called to tell me that there's been an outbreak of head lice in George's second grade classroom and, unfortunately, George is one of those afflicted. I'm mortified. When I was a child growing up, we only heard about one or two cases of head lice, and it was very clear that it was something that never happened in "good" families.

I listen numbly as the nurse tells me what I have to do. I'm shaking as I hang up the phone and dial Dr. DiNicola's office, asking them to please call in a prescription shampoo to the pharmacy in Barre. As soon as all of the kids are home, I pile them into our van and we head in to town to pick it up.

******

"I'm going to die!" I yell as Hector comes into the kitchen. The sight in front of him must be shocking, I think, and suddenly I burst into tears. I'm standing at the sink in my bra and panties scrubbing Joelle's head under a spray of hot water. The rest of the kids are shivering around the table, stripped down to their underwear.

"What in the world…?" he asks.

"Lice!" I scream.

"Calm down and tell me what's going on and what you need me to do," he says.

I explain the instructions I received from the nurse. Every person in the house has to be shampooed with Quell, for a full three minutes, in hot water. Every item of clothing in the house has to be washed and dried on the hottest cycle. All of the towels and bedding have to be washed, and all the stuffed animals and pillows put into plastic bags and not taken out for three weeks. The furniture has to be sprayed. And then we have to comb everyone out with this special little metal comb.

"You've got to be kidding me," Hector says in disbelief.

"Do I look like I'm kidding?" I shriek. "I'm going insane here. Joelle's shampoo is last —I've been scrubbing heads for an hour under scalding water. My hands are numb. I haven't even started the laundry. That's why the kids have no clothes on. I can't handle this."

"I'll work on the laundry," he offers. "I'll get at least one load done quickly with PJs for everyone so they can get something on."

"Thanks. But you have to strip down and shampoo yourself first," I tell him. I'll get the PJs going while you do that. Then you can help with the combing out—I haven't even started that part yet. We have to figure out some dinner, too."

******

"I'm glad we're done with that project, Sue," Hector says when we finally fall into bed—on our sheetless mattress, with no blankets—at three in the morning. "If another kid ever comes home with head lice again, I'm going to shave all their heads, even the girls."

"Yeah, they'll love that," I say. "We'll be known as the 'Baldie' family instead of the Badeau family.

******

Head lice plagued us repeatedly for months after that. We never did shave heads, although Hector's mother did cut SueAnn, Chelsea, and Flory's hair quite short one day when she was helping us after another lice outbreak. At the time, it was the most stressful event of my life. Little could I imagine that the day would come when I'd laugh about it.

I walk into the kitchen with the mail in my hands. "You must have been busy today. You left the mail in the mailbox," I say to Hector.

"Yeah, a lot of laundry today," he says. "Why, anything special in the mail?"

"As a matter of fact, there is. Look at this."

"Vermonter of the Year?" he says. "How did that happen?" "Read the rest of the letter. One of our volunteers at Rootwings wrote a letter nominating us and we were selected. It's based on our work with Rootwings and the kids we have adopted. I'm pretty overwhelmed."

"Wow, that is really something. It's pretty funny," Hector muses. "It seems that some people think we are completely crazy and others think we are saints. No one seems to believe we are just a normal family trying to live out our faith one day at a time."

"Well, it says here that they will do an article on us in the *Vermont Sunday* magazine. Maybe we can convince them we are normal," I laugh. "And if not, at least maybe the article will inspire a few other people to adopt some kids too."

"Yeah, as long as it helps kids, it's worth it. But when will the interview be? We leave for New Mexico in four days," he reminds me.

******

After going back and forth with the social workers all fall, they have decided to approve our family to adopt the youngest of the six teen siblings. We'll travel to New Mexico next week to meet David, who's deaf, and bring him home with us to Vermont. We're hoping while we're there to at least meet the other five. We know the older kids have more say in whether or not they want to be adopted, but maybe once they meet us they will be interested in our family.

******

"Now boarding. US Air flight to Burlington, Vermont."

"Let's go, Renee and Trish," Hector says, "That's our flight." He motions for David to join us and slings a backpack across his shoulders.

As we board the plane, we notice Vermont's governor seated in First Class. We greet her, and she agrees to take a photo of us with our newest family members once we land in Vermont.

"We did it, Hec," I say. "We convinced the muckety-mucks that Renee and Trish still need a family."

"Not bad," he replies, "We're batting .500 on this trip. I'm glad we got to meet all of the kids. It's too bad Lilly missed the going-away party for David at the School for the Deaf, but I'm glad we got to meet her when we visited Hobbs."

"Yeah, thankfully we survived our ride on the crazy little plane. What were there—ten seats on it? That was worse than a roller-coaster ride," I say. He knows how much I hate amusement park rides.

"Well, at least we got their worker to agree to bring Fisher, Lilly, and JD to Vermont for a visit next month. This way at least they will have a chance to see where their siblings are and get to know our family a little better. Who knows what will happen after that?"

"I'm looking forward to that. In the meantime, I have all the arrangements made with the Austine School for the Deaf to get David started, but since we didn't know Trish and Renee were coming, I'm starting from square one with Spaulding."

"You'll get some interesting looks and comments when you register Trish and Renee. There are quite a few teachers, and the assistant principal, still there from when we were students. They might have a hard time figuring out how we managed to have teenagers so soon—and black teenagers at that!"

"Not to mention Coach Poirier. He's still coaching hockey, you know. Yeah, that will be the first of many experiences I'm sure we will have on this newest leg of our journey," I say.

******

We arrive at home and eight of the kids come tumbling out the porch door, nearly knocking us down in their excitement. Mamere, who was babysitting, is waiting in the living room with Raj and

Joelle. The kids are especially eager to try out their sign language skills on David. We've been taking lessons from a couple, Dennis and Jean, who are fluent signers and also recently adopted an older child through Rootwings. As each child tries to out-do each other with their signing skills, they eventually get around to taking David upstairs to show him his new room. When Hector, Trish, Renee, and I catch up with his entourage, David is standing in the middle of his room, looking at all of his new siblings and making the sign for family over and over. I catch Hector's eyes and notice that his, like mine, are brimming with tears.

This is our first glimpse of David's contagious smile, optimistic spirit, and hard-working readiness to jump in to new experiences with both feet. It's no wonder that we'll soon be calling him our "family ambassador."

Chapter Ten
JD, Fisher, and Lilly

"Can you believe this snow?" I say to Hector, "Of all days, a real nor'easter has to hit the day they're coming. But I just got off the phone with US Air and they say the flight is still coming in, so I guess I better start heading up to Burlington."

"Just drive slowly. You'll be all right," he says, "Trish! Renee! If you still plan to go to the airport with Mom, come on. It's time to go!"

******

We've had more than a few cups of hot chocolate at the small Burlington airport, but sure enough, their flight is landing. I see them walking toward us before they see me, and I can tell that they are all shocked to see a whirlwind of whiteness just outside the window. All three of them, and Nancy, their worker, are wearing very "hip" and decidedly un-wintery clothes. After our initial greetings, they wait for their luggage while I go to a pay phone to call Hector and let him know they finally landed.

"You should get a room in a hotel there in Burlington and drive home tomorrow, Sue," he says.

"No, it wasn't that bad on the way up—as long as I went slow. We'll be fine," I say.

"Well, it's still snowing like crazy here," he adds. "We've got at least 16 inches of fresh snow since you left and more on the way."

"We'll be fine."

******

Driving slowly, following the plow as often as I can, I'm confident we'll make it home. Nancy is sitting in the front, looking a little shell-shocked about the situation. JD, Fisher, and Lilly are in the back peppering Renee and Trish with questions about life in Vermont. "Are there any other black kids at your high school?" Lilly asks.

"Yeah, a few," Renee says.

"No, not really," says Trish. "You know there are a few that look black, but they don't act black."

Finally, I'm making the turn from Lower Cabot onto the hill that leads to our house—just three miles to go. Less than a mile from the bottom, I can see that we're not going to make it, so I turn around and decide to go the longer way. It's a more gently sloping hill and I'm hopeful I'll get more traction. We're doing well until, about a mile from our house, a car is stuck crossways on the road and we can't go any further. We have to walk. I tell the kids they can leave their stuff in the van; it'll be locked and safe. But Fisher won't leave without his boom box.

******

"I'm freezing!" Lilly yells as she lurches into the house ahead of the others, waking up Hector, who's dozed on the couch.

"Quiet down, you knucklehead," JD says. "You want to wake up the dead?"

Nancy shakes snow from her clothes, and Fisher brushes snow off his boom box. Everyone huddles around the warmth of the Russian furnace.

"We had to start walking about a mile from here," I explain, but then Rusty came along in his truck and picked us up, so we're OK. We'll have to walk back in the morning to get the luggage."

"Well, I'm glad you all made it. I'll show you to your rooms so we can all get some sleep, and we can talk more in the morning," Hector says, whispering to me as we lead the way. "I told you to get a room!"

When we finally fall into bed, Hector gives me a quick kiss and says, "Well, this is off to a great start. I'm pretty sure they're *never* going to want to come back here again."

"Who knows?" I say, sleepily. "You never know what God has up his sleeve."

******

"Hey, JD," I hear Hector say while I'm making coffee the day before they're scheduled to head back to New Mexico. "I need to split up some wood outside, do you want to give me a hand?"

"Sure, Mr. Hector," he says, and both he and Fisher head out the door.

Several minutes later, the three of them come inside, and Hector says that they would like to talk to Nancy and I. "We've been thinking," JD begins.

"About your offer to include all of us in your family," Fisher adds. "JD and I would like that. We'd like to move up here. We were just talking to Mr. Hector about it. We want to be a family again with David and our sisters."

"The snow adventure didn't discourage you?" I say, somewhat in shock.

Nancy turns to Fisher, adding, "I know JD is out of school, but this is the last semester of your senior year. Are you sure you want to move three thousand miles across the country at this stage of your life?"

"To be reunited with my siblings, it's worth it," he says.

"What about Lilly?"

"She's not sure yet," JD says. "But we're ready."

******

"What time is it?" Hector says as we plop into bed.
"It's midnight."

"What a day. Can't believe JD and Fisher decided they want to join the family. What Fisher said about it being worth it to move three thousand miles even in his senior year of high school—that really touched me. Although I have to admit, I am a little scared. Do we really know what we are getting into? Those guys are both over six feet—they tower over me!"

"Don't worry, Hec. They're good kids. It'll be a great adventure. And our batting average just went up a few hundred points—five out of six of them are being reunited. What a blessing!"

"Let's get some sleep—love you."

"Love you too—good night."

******

Fisher has a car. So the plans are made for me to fly to New Mexico to meet up with him, pick up JD, and drive back. We'll have to drive straight through because I have an important licensing meeting for Rootwings that I can't miss. After saying good-bye to Lilly, we hit the road—JD, Fisher, and I each taking four-hour driving shifts with about 2,500 miles to cover.

As we cross from New Mexico into Texas, Fisher says to me, "I smoke, you know." And a few minutes later, "I sometimes drink a beer." I expected to be tested when parenting teens—the group home gave us plenty of practice—and this seems mild so far.

"Hector and I will work with you on that," I say. "We've been around the block with teenage boys. Nothing you do is going to surprise us or make us change our minds about welcoming you into our family. "

On the ride, I learn that Fisher feels he needs more time to complete high school, so we agree to enroll him as a junior instead of a senior. Since JD is out of school, I talk to him about working in our family book and packaging business and helping with the conference book sales. We have a big conference coming up in the Catskills, and I can really use his help. It's a new group called Families of Tomorrow. They met us at NACAC and asked us to be their official bookseller. They promise a couple of thousand attendees at their conference—this could really help our business grow!

When March rolls around, JD and I head for New York. We have a great time at the conference. He gets to meet a lot of my adoption friends, and we take a drive into the Big Apple one evening with our friends Brus and Diane and their daughter. While walking on 42nd Street we are surprised to see Bernadette Peters exit the stage door of one of the theatres. What a treat.

The conference, however, is a bust. We'd ordered a huge inventory of books and sold very few. The promised thousands of participants didn't materialize, and we're left holding the bag, along with all the other vendors who had been lured to the conference. As we pull into our driveway back in Cabot, I am worried about how we'll pay for all these books when the bills come due in thirty days. *Lord, I'm trusting you to provide a way—you just gave us five more mouths to feed. Please help us with the finances.*

That worry quickly evaporates as Hector comes to the door and says, "Batting a thousand!"

"What are you talking about?" I ask.

"Lilly called. She talked for a while with Trish, and then asked for you, but since you weren't here, she settled for me," he jokes. "She says she wants to come join her family after all. I told her you will call Nancy tomorrow and make the travel arrangements. She heard we enrolled Fisher as a junior and she wants to do that too. She'd like one more year of high school."

"Wow, what brought that about?"

"She didn't really say, but basketball season is over and she wants to make the move before track season begins."

"Interesting. God sure does work in mysterious ways. After all these years apart, they will now be together . . . That's so awesome!"

******

"I have some cool news, Hec."

"What's that?"

"Well, I just got off the phone with Nancy in New Mexico. I fly out there on Thursday, sign all the papers and fly home with Lilly on Friday. And it seems that the only seats left on the flight she is arranging for Lilly and I are in first class. I've never flown first class before. I'm psyched!"

******

"How can I know that we can really trust you? What makes you different than all the other families who made promises to us and then let us down?" Lilly is questioning me just as soon we are settled into our comfy, first class seats.

"We've made a commitment to you, you're part of our family now. That commitment is just as serious to us as the marriage vows Hector and I said to each other nine years ago when we got married—'for better and for worse.' We feel the same way about adoption. We're making a commitment not only to you but also to God, and with his help we intend to keep it. It doesn't matter what you do—get pregnant, go to jail, get hooked on drugs, drop out of school—no matter what happens, you are our family, we are your parents and we'll all be in this together."

Little did I know that every single thing on my list of 'worst-case scenarios' would come true within the next 10 years. But I did know that God would walk this path with us every step of the way.

******

"Great job, Fisher and Lilly," Hector says as we walk towards the parking lot at Spaulding. "I'm not an expert on track, but you left everyone else in the dust—that was amazing."

"Thanks. There was a lot more competition in New Mexico," Lilly says. "I think we'll do OK here in Vermont, but that wasn't my best time."

"Looked great to me," Hector says, "And Fisher, your long jump was incredible. You really took it to them."

As we approach the vehicles, Fisher and Lilly head for Fisher's car, Hector and I, along with our crew of little kids, walk toward the van. "Can we ride home with Fisher?" Renee asks

"If it's OK with him," I say.

"Don't forget, mud season has hit—watch yourself on our hill, Fish," Hector cautions.

******

We arrive home before the kids and our answering machine light is flashing. As I retrieve the messages, one is from Marialisa Calta from the *New York Times*. They saw the Vermonter of the Year article on our family, and they want to do an article on us.

"Hec, listen to this message—the *New York Times*! Can you believe that?"

"Wow—all this publicity. It is a little much. Not sure how to react," he says.

"This will bring national attention to kids who need homes," I say.

"As long as we remember our purpose and calling. It's to help kids find homes and give the glory to God—not to us."

"I know, we have to be careful not to let it go to our heads, but be thankful for the opportunity."

Just then, Renee comes storming into the house with Trish close behind her. "What's going on?" I ask.

"Fisher got his car stuck in the mud," Renee answers. "Him and JD are trying to get it out, but its only getting worse. We decided to walk home, but Lilly didn't want to ruin her shoes so she's sitting in the car,".

"How far down the hill?" Hector asks.

"Down by the flat part before the steep part," Trish says.

"Oh, half a mile or so. OK, I'll go give them a hand."

******

"You should have seen the mess they were in," Hector says after he steps out of the shower. "When I was walking toward the car, they were cussing a blue streak, but as soon as they saw me, it stopped. I guess they have a little respect and discretion. Anyway, it took a lot of pushing, and we all were covered in mud, but we made it. What a mess—now Fisher is outside washing his car."

"Hmmmph," I say. "That's a losing battle during mud season!"

******

_"Another stack of mail came today," Hector tells me as I come in from Barre; he has a pile of envelopes in his hand. I ride to and from Rootwings with Fisher and Lilly now, and my schedule revolves around their school and track schedule. Every day since the *New York Times* article appeared, we have received phone calls and mail. Most are from people interested in adopting, or some who want to donate to Rootwings. The phone at the office has been ringing off the hook, too.

"It's so exciting to see the response—exactly what we prayed for. So many children are going to get families," I say, just as the phone rings.

******

"You can't begin to imagine who that was," I say when I get off the phone. "It was Lucie Arnaz—you know, the daughter of Lucille Ball and Desi Arnaz. She is in the hospital recuperating from something and she read the article about our family. She and her husband want to come to Vermont and meet us."

"Yeah right. And she wants to sell us a bridge in Brooklyn too, right?" Hector says, not quite believing me.

"No, really. It was *her*."

"Well, you'll have to tell me all about it when I get back. I have to leave with Jose, Abel, and SueAnn for Little League practice. I cooked up some burgers—the little kids ate already. You and Fisher and Lilly can have what's left. Oh, and Flory has a homework assignment she needs a little help with—in math, I saved it for you."

******

Lucie and Larry decided to come visit on a day when Lilly has a basketball game. They agree to join us at the game and then we go out to dinner at a local diner in Barre before we head home back to Cabot and they leave for the airport in Burlington. Earlier, they spent the day meeting all of our other kids at our house. They've invited us to visit them in California next time we take a summer trip, and they promise to explore other ways to support our family efforts to find homes for waiting children.

"You just never know what is around the next curve in the road," Hector says.

The phone is ringing as we enter the house. It's JD. He has been detained by the police in Barre. "What? Are you kidding? Let me talk to the officer—what's his name? Oh brother, I know him," Hector says, taking the phone.

"Yes, he's our son, and yes, he has friends in that neighborhood. What did he do that caused you to detain him?"

******

"What's going on?" I ask.

"I guess racism is alive and well in Barre," Hector says, shaking his head. "You know that policeman everyone calls Chooch? He's arrested my brother a few times when he got into fights after drinking. Well anyway, he detained JD for no reason at all except for parking his car in a neighborhood where it 'looked like he didn't belong,' according to Chooch. I'd like to wring his scrawny neck." Needless to say, Hector is steaming.

"That probably won't help. I knew our kids would face some racism, but I didn't expect it in the town where we grew up and everyone knows us." I'm shaking my head. "Who knows what other issues we will encounter?"

******

The kitchen is a disaster. Hector and I have been outside enjoying the warm spring evening and chatting with our neighbor when we hear a crash in the kitchen. A trail of spilled juice leads from the kitchen to the playroom. Peanut butter is smeared on the counter and shards from a couple of broken plates are strewn on the floor. We hear Raj crying in the playroom.

"Everyone get in the kitchen, right now!" Hector yells. The kids come running in, doing their best to look innocent. "What happened here?" No one comes forward.

I go to Raj and pick him up, comforting him, as he says, "He hit me, kicked me, pulled my hair."

"Who?" I ask. Raj doesn't reply.

"I will give you one minute to step up and tell me what happened, or else it will be early bed for everyone," Hector says. After waiting a minute, he begins to count down: "Ten, nine, eight, seven . . . "

"I made the mess," Jose says. "I was making the juice and I spilled it, then I dropped the plates. And then I went in the playroom and started bugging Raj."

No one else says a word. "Is that right?" Hector asks, looking into each child's face. "That's the whole story? OK, Jose, you stay in here and clean up and then you have half an hour early bed."

"Jose didn't do all that by himself, you know," I say to Hector as we walk out of the room to get Joelle and Todd ready for bed.

"I know that. He always wants to take the consequences when no one else steps forward. We have to figure out a way to break that pattern."

******

Now it's my turn to be furious. Barre City School district has sent us a certified letter billing us for thousands of dollars of tuition, and saying that we can't send Fisher, Lilly, Renee, or Trish to Spaulding next year since we live in Cabot. We had advocated for them to attend Spaulding when they first arrived, feeling that they would adjust better in the larger high school with more academic and sports options than in Cabot's small school. Although everyone was agreeable for the rest of this school year, they have now reversed course.

"We can fight this, Sue. But to tell you the truth, I've been thinking that we should consider moving into Barre. It's not just the teenagers, but also our doctors, our grocery store, the Rootwings office. . . . It's just a lot to have to drive back and forth all the time, especially when the roads are bad."

"I hate to give up this house and land," I say. "And all the younger kids are doing so well here, I hate to uproot them."

"I know there are lots of great memories here. Like going out into the back woods with the kids to get our Christmas tree every year. Chelsea's first day of kindergarten. Or running races with JD and Fisher and Doug when he visited. JD always scrambling to make an excuse when Fisher beat him. And then the *Woman's Day* article and how they made that funny family photo, sticking Fisher and Lilly in the window when they weren't really here at the time. "

"All the birthday parties and cookouts," I add. "And the kids decorating their bikes for the Fourth of July parade. Making sopapaillas for Flory's class. Raj and Joelle and Todd all learned to walk here. The clubhouse in the back, and the year you made the playroom as the special Christmas gift—an indoor sandbox, jungle gym, ballet barre—we'll never replace that. All the kids putting on plays, Abel and George making tree forts, picking rhubarb and making pie, skiing out the back door . . . "

"Yeah, and the time Jose was skiing with Earl and Ricky and they skied over the top of his head!"

"That was a great memory?" I ask.

"Well, it's a memory, maybe not so great, but funny now. Or the time Isaac jumped

out the window of his second-floor bedroom trying to be Superman—how many stitches did he need? And the day you were so mad you started breaking plates."

"Lilly breaking the window on the van . . . SueAnn getting hit in the head with a baseball bat at Abel's game, or the day we got called because JD had driven his car into the river . . . "

By now, tears are rolling down our cheeks we are laughing so hard. "I'll miss this place. But you're right, I think we do need to move to Barre. At least we have a friend from church who is a Realtor; she won't swindle us, and we can trust her. I'll call her in the morning," I say.

"When we bought this house, I thought I would grow old and die here," Hector says. "And be buried in the backyard. But I can see now that this was just a stepping-stone on the road God has for us. Not sure what the next phase will look like, but like Doug always says in Bible study, 'When you take it to the Lord in prayer, be prepared to be surprised by His answer.'"

Roots and Wings at Loonstone Lake

Volume 1 - Call of the Loon

Prologue

July 11, 1974

"Shhhhhhh, do you hear that?" Twelve-year-old Louanne Thomas stopped dead in her tracks as she waited for her cousin Christopher and best friend Molly Mears to catch up to her.

"Hear what?" Chris called out.

Breathing. Giggles. Faster breathing, almost panting. And then—crying?

Molly's eyes widened. "Someone's in there," she said, motioning to the abandoned cabin they had come to explore. "Someone's crying in there."

Chris began flicking his flashlight from side to side. Louanne grabbed his hand, forcing him to stop. "Cut it out, Chris, we don't want to be seen. I can't imagine who could be in there, I didn't see any other boat when we pulled ashore, did you?"

"No other boats on this side of the island," Chris said. "Maybe whoever it is swam over."

"That would be a long swim in the dark."

"Maybe someone lives here," Molly suggested.

"In that old abandoned cabin? Huh, I doubt it," Louanne replied. "Besides they'd still have to get on and off the island for food."

"Then maybe its haunted. Baaahaaaahaaaa!" Chris said, holding his flashlight under his chin and making a menacing face.

"We should get out of here," Molly said.

"No way. We came here to check out that old cabin, and that's what I plan to do. This makes it even better!"

"Chris, you're being so loud. We're not s'posed to be here, remember? I don't know about you, but I don't want to be grounded for the rest of the summer," Louanne said, adding, "but I would like to check it out more. Let's go back to the edge of the water and walk around to the other side of the island—you know the side where the cabin has that broken window. Maybe we'll see something."

The three youngsters scrambled back down to the spot where they'd tied up their canoe and began creeping silently toward the other side of the island.

"Look there." This time it was Chris who stopped in his tracks, pointing to a boat moored between two rocks, "Isn't that Uncle Charlie's boat?"

Coming up alongside her cousin, Louanne took a good look at the boat. "Sure is," she said, "Can't miss that stupid mermaid he painted on the side of it. What the heck is he doing here?"

No sooner were those words out of her mouth than the cabin door opened and Uncle Charlie emerged, taking quick strides toward his boat. Someone else was with him.

"Who is that?"

"Shhhhh"

"I can't tell. But we better hope he doesn't see us." All three flattened themselves against the damp sand, hoping they could become invisible.

Uncle Charlie didn't look their way. He and his mystery partner slipped quietly into his boat and pushed off. Soon the rhythmic sounds of his paddles dipping into the water grew dimmer as the boat smoothly glided towards the Loon's Nest campground.

Chapter One

May 7, 2014

"That hit the spot," Frank Hubert said, picking up his empty plate and walking towards the kitchen sink. "I'll wash these dishes and then I have to start grading those senior essays."

"Great. I have to run an errand before I can finish the stack of papers I'm working on tonight. Do you need anything from the market?" Louanne asked her husband as she grabbed the car keys off the hook by the door and snatched her purse from the end table.

"Just sugar for my coffee."

Forty minutes later, Louanne walked into her kitchen balancing three bags of groceries and calling out, "I'm back." She quickly put the items away and sighed as she looked at the clock. Already eight o'clock and so many papers to grade. Another late night ahead.

As she entered their shared study, Frank looked up and said, "Your cousin Christopher called while you were out. We chatted a bit about the kids' college plans and whatnot, but it sure sounded like he was calling with a mission he couldn't discuss with me. He wants you to call him back tonight if you can."

"That's odd," Louanne replied. "Chris never calls. I can't think of a time we talked by phone, except when he called to let us know Uncle Walt died last year. I sure hope no one else has died."

"I don't think so. He sounded serious but not upset or sad."

"Hmmmm, OK, well I guess I'll call him back now before I get my head into these papers. Are you making any progress on yours?"

"These are done," Frank said, pointing to a pile of papers to his left, and then indicating the pile on his right, added, "These are not. I'll get us both some tea and then I'll get back to it. Maybe you can make your call from the porch. It's pleasant out there tonight."

Louanne was just ending her call with her cousin when Frank strolled onto the porch. "That was a long call—must have been serious," he noted. "I just came to see if you needed a refill on your tea."

"Oh shoot, I didn't even drink my tea," Louanne said. "Did you finish your papers already?"

"Well, not sure if I'd call it 'already,'—it is after nine. And yes, I finished, so I'm ready to kick back and watch the rest of the ball game before hitting the sack. But I thought I'd check on you first."

"After nine? Ugh. I'm going to have to get up extra early to grade my papers. My head is spinning now and I'm too tired to read sixty-five renditions on the similarities and differences between *Romeo and Juliet* and *West Side Story*. Can you sit out here with me for a few minutes before you watch the game? I want to tell you about my call with Chris." Louanne said, shooing Inky off the porch chair next to her.

"Anything for you, dear," Frank chuckled, taking the proffered seat as the cat jumped back up and landed on his lap.

"Chris wants to sell Loon's Nest." Louanne stated. She tried to sound matter of fact, but tears sprang to her eyes suddenly as a vivid memory of sitting on the porch of Ramy and Popi's cabin at the lake flooded her mind. "I know I haven't mentioned Loon's Nest in years. Truthfully, I haven't even thought about it in years. But now, the idea of it being gone, not being in the family anymore, that's a little overwhelming."

Frank wisely gave Louanne a few quiet moments with her thoughts. The Loon's Nest Campground at Loonstone Lake in northern New England had been in her family for as long as she could remember. Her grandparents, George and Hazel Thomas, spent every summer up there, living in the family cottage and renting out the other eight cabins to families and fishermen from around the country. Their three sons, Louanne's father Henry, and his brothers, Uncle Walt and Uncle Charlie, had worked at the campground every summer of their youth, and when Henry and Walt went off to the Korean War, and Popi George died, Uncle Charlie managed it himself. Louanne, along with her siblings and cousins spent their summers barefoot and bronzed, playing in the lake, canoeing, hiking in the woods and waiting for their turn to become official Loon's Nest staffers when they turned fifteen.

Louanne smiled as she remembered feeling so small sitting in the big green Adirondack chairs on the front lawn, watching her daddy and uncles cleaning their fishing gear while the ladies played croquet. Her grandmother Hazel, called "Ramy" because her firstborn grandchild Christopher couldn't pronounce "Grammy," loved playing croquet even after she could no longer walk. Uncle Charlie faithfully pushed her around the lawn in her wheelchair so she could continue to beat anyone who challenged her to a game.

But then, in 1974, everything changed. The camp closed mid-summer, Uncle Charlie moved out west and no one talked about the camp again. The memories were packed up along with the photographs, croquet mallets and canoe paddles and locked in the attic of the family cottage at Loonstone Lake.

"What brought this on now?" Frank asked, coaxing her out of her reverie.

"College tuition," Louanne stated. "When the camp closed down in 1974, Daddy and Uncle Walt arranged for it to be put into a trust for Chris and I as the two oldest grandchildren. Chris said he never wanted to do anything with it as long as his dad was alive, but now that Uncle Walt has been gone for a year, he considers the camp to be 'the family albatross' and he says it would be good stewardship to sell it and use the funds for more important things. Like college tuition for his kids."

"The 'family albatross?' That's a pretty harsh statement. I thought you all had fond memories of your time at the camp when you were kids?" Frank probed.

"We did. I do. But no one knows what happened in 1974 and we just all understood it was never to be talked about while our parents were alive. And now that they're dead, who can we ask?"

Frank quietly reached for Louanne's hand, "Childhood memories. Potent stuff. I hope our kids have nothing but positive memories of the camping trips we took with them. Remember the time we were at Yellowstone and the bear came through our tent site?"

Louanne laughed, "I'm not sure Sidney has fond memories of that one. Luke and Robby really had him convinced the bear was going to eat him for breakfast." Now the tears streaming down her face were happy ones as memories of good times with Frank and their four children camping around the country began rolling across her mind, one after another, like gentle waves lapping the side of a canoe. "I wonder how their memories would have been different if we had camped in one place every year—you know, like the Loon's Nest—instead of taking those trips around the country?"

"I have an idea!" Frank said, "Let's tell Chris that we want to spend one last weekend at the lake before we join him in putting it on the market. We could go up for Memorial Day. We need a getaway and it would be fun. It would give you a chance to re-live some of your favorite memories and say goodbye to the camp. You know, that whole closure thing you always tell me is so important?"

"Oh what a great idea. Frank! Maybe we'll find some records of my family history up there—maybe even learn what really happened in 1974."

"Who knows what we will find? Mostly I hope we'll find some time with each other. The cots in the cabin have to be more comfortable then the air mattresses we slept on when camping with the kids." Frank added with a wink, "But for now, let's get some sleep. The ball game is over and five A.M. will roll around all too soon."

Chapter Two

May 23, 2014

"Wow! It's beautiful Lou-lou," Frank said, stepping out of the van and opening his arms expansively to take in the full picture of the campground before him.

Louanne's face did not mirror Frank's. In place of his broad smile, she grimaced. "Oh Frank, I'm not sure what I expected. I guess I was expecting it to still be the way it looked when I was a little girl." The broken windows, upended Adirondack chairs and lawn that looked like a hayfield were almost too much to take in.

"Yes, I hope Chris understands how much work it's going to take to get this place in shape to sell. But honey—the lake, the evergreens, the maples. It's spectacular. Wow, I wish you had brought me here years ago, I can just envision camping here with the kids."

Louanne barely heard him as she wandered away from the family cottage and headed towards the rental cabins. Each cabin was named for a tree. Elm. Maple. Spruce. Hemlock. Balsam. Poplar. Birch. And her favorite, Larch. Walking the rocky shore path, she noticed that some of the cabins still had canoes tethered to trees, while others were long gone. The canoe in front of Balsam had become a home for some kind of animal—raccoons maybe? And the one by Birch was cracked and broken, but hanging on.

"Cracked and broken, but hanging on. That should be the new theme song for the Loon's Nest Campground," Louanne mused aloud to herself as she stepped around behind Larch and into the woods, looking for the staff cabins. The path that had been there was completely overgrown, so she was picking her way through based on memories that were decades old. "Can it really have been forty years since I was last here?"

Louanne was feeling a little disoriented and lost when she heard Frank calling to her from the family cottage, "Lou-lou where did you go? We should get a few things unpacked before it gets dark." Still not finding the staff cabins, she was thankful to see Larch again.

"I must have walked in a circle," she said to herself, shaking her head. She decided to head back to where Frank was waiting for her.

As soon as Louanne stepped into the opening where the family van was parked, she saw Frank setting up the tent they'd tossed in at the last minute, "just in case" they needed it. "The floorboards are warped and dangerous in there, Lou, and there are mice droppings everywhere and some bigger droppings—maybe deer—in the kitchen. I think we'll be better off in the tent for tonight. Maybe tomorrow we can clean up at least one cabin enough to make it our base for the rest of the weekend."

"Oh, it's that bad? I should have known."

"It's OK, it's still beautiful and peaceful. We've camped in tents for years; one more night won't kill us. Can you give me a hand here, hold the stakes while I pound them in?"

An hour later, after establishing a relatively comfortable little campsite, Frank and Louanne decided to take a walk and explore the rest of Loon's Nest. The sun was beginning to set over the lake as they approached the waterfront. "Listen Frank," Louanne stood stock-still inclining her ear towards the lake. The hauntingly beautiful sounds took her breath away.

"Are we hearing the loons?" Frank, too, stood still, listening, mesmerized. "I haven't heard loons since that time we camped in northern Minnesota with Jack and Diane. Emily was just two that summer. They had just adopted their Justin and that's when we first thought about adopting, remember? Wow—so long ago! But I'll never forget that loon music."

"Come here, Frank." Louanne grabbed his hand and led him through a stand of trees towards the water. Where they stepped out from the trees, a large boulder jutted into the water. "This is my prayer rock. My grandmother, Ramy Hazel, she was the spiritual head of the family. She was the one who never let us go to bed without a Bible story, and she was up at the crack of dawn every morning reading her own worn-out Bible and praying for all of us. Ramy told me to find a place where I felt comfortable talking to God and then to visit Him there everyday. This was my place." Louanne dropped Frank's hand and climbed onto the rock. Frank stood back and snapped a picture.

"Such peace here," she continued. "I'd sit and pray and I always felt like the loons were singing their own hymns to God. Silly, I guess, but oh, how I've missed this place."

"I can see why it holds such a special place in your heart. I'm looking forward to exploring it more in the morning. Maybe one of these old canoes is still sturdy enough for us to go out onto the lake. We could paddle over to that island and back." Frank pointed across the lake to an island with a ramshackle house on it. "It looks like that house is abandoned."

Louanne followed his gaze to the island and shivered.

"What is it?"

"I'm not sure. Something about that island creeps me out. Chris and I used to paddle out there as kids, but, I don't know, something is tickling at the back of my mind. It will probably come to me."

The next morning Frank was busy brewing coffee on the camp cook stove by the time Louanne woke up. "Good morning sleepy head," he said, handing her a steaming mug, with a giant grin on his face and a twinkle in his eyes. Louanne knew he was up to something.

"What?" she asked suspiciously, raising an eyebrow and lightly blowing on the hot coffee.

"I couldn't sleep, so I walked down to your prayer rock and sat there for hours last night. I don't think I slept at all, I'm so excited."

"You sure look chipper for someone who didn't sleep. What's all the excitement about? I'm feeling a little sad myself. Being here makes me realize how much I love this place and it's making it harder to think about letting go of it."

"Let's take that canoe ride and I'll tell you my ideas," Frank said, pulling Louanne to her feet.

"Now?"

"No time like the present—Let's go!"

There was no sun on the lake; the slate color of the sky nearly matched the color of the water. As they climbed into the canoe, Louanne spotted the family of loons hugging the shoreline about a hundred yards away. "Did you know that loons are monogamous and mate for life?" she asked Frank.

"Really?"

"Yup. Learned that from Popi George. He was a hunter and fisherman and knew everything about the wildlife here at the lake. He also taught me that in loon families, the momma loons and poppa loons share equally in the responsibility of raising the young. Fascinating, isn't it?" Just then a powerful adult loon burst into the air and executed a spectacular dive below the surface of the water.

Frank paddled mid-way across the lake and then sat still. Louanne listened to the rhythmic slapping of the water against the side of the boat, waiting for Frank to share his ideas. From this vantage point, they could see the entire Loon's Nest Campground and half a dozen of the privately owned homes along the edge of the lake.

"I've been thinking about that favorite saying of yours. The one you embroidered on that wall-hanging before we adopted Robby and Sidney, 'There are only two lasting gifts we give our children – roots and wings.' – did I get it right?"

"Close enough." Louanne leaned towards Frank; the canoe rocked gently.

"We've always tried to help our kids know their roots—their birth family heritage—and roots in faith and in our family. But this place, this place represents your roots. We need to save it. It's your legacy. Let's keep it in the family! I was thinking instead of joining with Chris to sell it, we should buy out his half and keep it, rebuild it, reopen it. I have so many ideas about what we could do here—to use this place for new generations to grow deep roots and to spread their wings. Strong wings—like our friend the loon there."

"Oh Frank, I'd love to keep it in the family! But our kids are kind of past the camping stage now. Sid's in college and Robby, Luke and Em are busy with their lives, they aren't going to drop everything to come run a campground with us. And thank goodness there aren't any grandchildren just yet. So I'm not sure what you are thinking."

Frank began paddling back towards the shore. "You know how we always worry about those kids in our classes who have no family, no guidance? The kids in foster care, or the ones that have spent time in detention? They can't get summer jobs as easily as the other kids and they just seem adrift? What if we could develop a program for them? Job training. Life skills. We could hire them and save the camp at the same time."

Louanne burst into tears.

"What?" A look of bewilderment quickly replaced the exuberant smile on Frank's face.

"Oh Frank. You never knew my Popi George, but he would be so proud of you right now. He always hired what he called, 'troubled kids' to work here at the camp. If my dad said it once, he said it a million times, Popi's favorite quote was 'An honest day's work for an honest day's pay is the best way to help a kid get on the right path.' I love this idea!"

They spent the rest of the weekend sweeping, scrubbing, cleaning, dreaming and praying. By the time they got in the van to travel home on Monday afternoon, Louanne and Frank were convinced it was not only their plan, but God's own plan for them to buy out and reopen Loon's Nest.

"Just a few hurdles in our way, Frank." Louanne said as they turned off the dirt road and onto the highway, "Convincing our own kids that this is a good idea. Then convincing Chris and my siblings and other cousins." She began ticking off the challenges on her fingers.

"And don't forget coming up with the money," Frank added helpfully, "A boatload of money."

"Do you think we can pull it off? It seems impossible."

"*Impossible!*" Frank began to sing, belting out the song from the movie version of Cinderella, "*For a plain yellow pumpkin . . .* "

"*To become a golden carriage,*" Louanne joined in with a newfound lightness in her heart.

Chapter Three

May 31, 2014

"Sid's here!" Frank shouted up to Louanne as she finished dressing. She heard him dash out the front door, letting it slam in his wake. Both Louanne and Frank were eager to see their youngest son, he hadn't been home from college since Christmas break.

Louanne stepped into the kitchen just in time to be swept up into a bear hug. After the embrace, she pulled back and looked her tall, thin son up and down. "Most kids gain ten pounds in college, Sid, how did you manage to lose weight? I'm going to have to fatten you up while you're home. And this must be Liam," Louanne said, turning to the young man standing inside the doorway. "Come on in, I promise not to bite."

"Very nice to meet you, ma'am," the short, stocky young man with a flock of freckles and a shock of unruly red hair stuck his hand out awkwardly towards Louanne.

"No need to call me ma'am, although I will let your momma know that she raised you right! We're so glad you and Sid got this internship together for the summer. We're delighted to have you staying with us."

Frank and the two younger men gathered at the kitchen table where Louanne had placed a bowl of fruit and a basket of muffins. "Coffee?" Frank asked, filling four mugs. Louanne stood at the counter deveining the shrimp for her famous Shrimp and Avocado salad.

Within the hour, the other three Hubert children began arriving for the family's delayed Memorial Day barbeque.

"Need any help, Mom?" Luke asked as he fished a few grapes out of the fruit salad.

"I need your help making sure there is food for everyone else," Louanne replied, gently slapping her son's hand. "And yes, you can help. Can I get you to cut up some peppers and onions to throw on the grill? The grilled veggies go so well with the chicken. I need to put the punch together and then I think we are all set. Wonder why Emily's not here yet?"

"She texted me. She's on her way. She stopped to get ice cuz she knows you never have any," Luke said.

"Oh, I think I hear her car now. Did she say she was bringing anyone with her?"

"If you mean like Cory, the answer is no. They are not that serious mom. I think her friend Mealea is coming, though."

As if on cue, Emily and her best friend walked through the door, Em with bags of ice, and Mealea with a large Tupperware container. "I brought homemade spring rolls Mom-Lou," Mealea said, setting the container on the counter. "Half are vegan, you know, for Sid and whoever else wants vegan."

"Bless you," Louanne said, stepping around the counter to hug both girls.

"So, I can't believe we have a lakefront property in the family and we never knew about it. Spill the beans now, Mom. Dad." Robby said once everyone's plates were piled high with food and grace had been said.

"Yeah, spill now cuz you got a lot of 'splainin' to do," Luke added in his best Ricky Ricardo imitation.

"My grandparents owned a camp way up in a corner of northern New England called the 'Northeast Kingdom' for years and years. I spent my summers there as a child, with my siblings Karen and Brian and my cousins Chris and Janey. It was really like a piece of heaven," Louanne started. Looking at Mealea she added, "My best friend Molly used to come up there most summers, too."

"Your mom doesn't really know what happened, but the camp was closed down in the middle of the season long before any of you were a twinkle in the eye," Frank continued. "No one has used the camp since 1974, it has kind of lain fallow, but it has been held in a trust for your mom and her cousin Chris."

"Why did it close?"

"Was there a scandal?"

"All the camping we did, why didn't we go up there?"

The questions from their four adult children were flying fast and furious across the picnic table.

"After my Uncle Walt died last year, Chris started to think about selling the property. He figured the money could help him put his kids through college. So he called me to discuss it and that's when dad and I decided to go make a 'goodbye' pilgrimage to the camp last weekend." Louanne picked up the story as unexpected tears threatened to spill down her cheeks.

"I saw how much your mom loved the place and I thought we should try to keep it in the family," Frank explained, adding, "It would mean buying out Chris's share. Scraping up the money will be tough, and it would mean less for other family activities, like helping you when your car breaks down. Again." Everyone looked at Robby on that note and laughed.

"So," Louanne piped up, regaining her composure, "we wanted to hear what you kids thought before we took the plunge. Although we have already talked to Geoff Lukens at the Teacher's Credit

Union about applying for a loan just to see what it would take. Chris got an appraisal done before he called me. Even though the property is in terrible shape, it is still valued at almost a million dollars, so, well, it's a lot to come up with."

"What did Geoff think?" Luke asked. Geoff's younger brother Eric was one of Luke's high school classmates. "I trust him."

"He advised us to develop a business plan. Map out how we foresee bringing the campground back to life, and what the market would be in both the near-term and down the road," Frank replied.

"Seems reasonable," Sid said. "Have you done that yet?"

"Geoff put us in touch with a young kid who specializes in business plans, his name is Deion Abernathy. We have an appointment next Tuesday," Louanne said.

"Deion's not a young kid, he's two years older than me. I went to school with his sister Diamond," Emily noted. "Deion is really smart, I might add."

"You have to hear the best part of your dad's plan," Louanne said.

"I want to create a business model that not only results in a top-of-the-line campground experience for our guests, but also provides a summer job program for youth with extra challenges in their lives. Teens who have been in foster care, or juvenile justice. Maybe teens with disabilities. I'd love you guys to help with that part of the plan and maybe serve as mentors."

"I know I'm not officially part of the family, but I think that's a brilliant plan, Poppa-Frank," Mealea said.

"You know you are part of the family, silly girl, and I do appreciate your input. What about the rest of you?" Frank looked into the faces of each of his children.

"Go for it!"

"I'd be worried about you and mom working too hard when you should be starting to enjoy life a little, but all-in-all, it sounds like a good plan."

"Can I come to the meeting with Deion?"

"When do we get to see this place?"

One by one, they each weighed in and the conversation lasted through dessert. By the time marshmallows were roasting over the coals, there was a clear consensus to go forward with the business plan and loan application.

******

Louanne curled up next to Frank in bed later that evening and said, "That went better than I thought. We didn't 'need' their permission, but it sure feels good to know they are all onboard. It makes me feel more confident that the loan will come through. I'm starting to believe this might be possible."

"We still have to convince your cousin. If he considers the camp an albatross, I wonder how he will feel about letting it stay in the family?" Frank asked.

"I've been wondering that, too. Maybe he knows more about what happened in 1974 than I do. He is two years older than me, he might have seen or heard more than I can remember. I'll call him in the morning."

Chapter Four

June 4, 2014

A mere hint of the sun was peeking out from between the two houses next door when Louanne took her morning coffee to the porch with time to spare before heading out for another day of teaching. She expected to be alone and was surprised to see Sid's friend Liam already out there, clickety-clacking away on the keyboard of his tablet.

"Good morning Liam, you're up bright and early."

"Yes ma'am, its my best time to think," He replied, looking startled.

"How are you liking the internship so far?"

"I love it. They're not just making us get coffee or sort mail. Some of my professors told us to look out for that. But they are giving us real work. It's pretty cool."

"That's wonderful, Liam. I'm so glad you and Sid became friends. He often likes to be the lone ranger, so this is new territory for him, and I thank you for sharing it."

"Yes, ma'am. I think I'll go get ready for work now. Nice talking to you." And with that, he stood to go inside the house. As he opened the door, Frank stepped out.

70

"Did you scare the boy off?" he asked.

"I hope not. But I was kind of hoping for a little time alone."

"OK, hint taken, I'll go back inside."

"No, stay. Let's talk for a few minutes. It's been quite a week and my head is spinning. I can't believe in the last few days we got all four of our kids, my cousins, my sister and brother to agree to the Loon's Nest plan. And that meeting with Deion yesterday—I just loved getting all of our ideas down on paper in a way that actually makes sense. It feels like God is really walking with us on this."

"I feel more like He's walking one step ahead of us and blazing the trail," Frank said. "And who knew that the hardest sell would be your brother, Brian. He doesn't even remember Loon's Nest, but he sure had lots of opinions about what should happen to it."

"Yea, that threw me too. Truthfully, I thought it would be Chris's sister Janey we'd have the most trouble with. She was always a little angry that Dad and Uncle Walt left the campground to Chris and I and not to all of the cousins equally."

"It was smart to suggest that we will pay each of your siblings and Janey a portion of the value in addition to Chris's share. Goodwill and peace for the family is always a good thing."

They sat quietly for a few moments, watching the sun splash streaks of butterscotch across the sky while three robins each staked out their hunting territories on the front lawn. A garbage truck rumbled by and two squirrels jumped from one branch to another in the neighbor's yard. Kyle Williams, the paperboy, tossed the daily onto the lawn and waved.

"What I'm most pleased about is Robby's interest in all of this," Frank picked up the discussion. "It was a big surprise that he wanted to come to the meeting with Deion, but he had such valuable input. I hope his enthusiasm continues."

"He really has a head for business and a heart for teens without families. He was only three when we adopted him, but it's almost like he can relate to them. In some ways, he is an old soul in a young man's body. Hard to believe he's only twenty-three."

Suddenly the door flew open as Sid and Liam dashed across the porch and down the steps to the car. Sid's hair was still wet and he was holding his tie with his teeth while he juggled car keys, tablet and briefcase with his two hands. Without so much as a nod or wave, the boys were in the car and on their way to their internship in town.

"Will that boy ever develop a sense of time?" Frank shook his head.

"Oh, he has a sense of time," Louanne answered, "It just doesn't match anyone else's."

"I suppose. Anyway, I guess that's our cue to get a move on, too. No slacking just because it's the last week of school. I'll drop our business plan and loan application off with Geoff after school while you attend that yearbook meeting and then I'll swing back over to school and pick you up."

******

"Can I help you with that?" Frank asked Imelda Collins.

"Oh thank you, dear. I don't see so well these days. Can't always tell where the curb is. Don't want to break my ankle like Lucy Bennett did last year. Poor thing." With Frank's help, the elderly woman successfully navigated the sidewalk by the church and got settled into her daughter's car.

"Thanks for helping out, Mr. Hubert," Tansey Collins called from the driver's side of the car. She had her hands full buckling two toddlers into car seats.

Stepping back, Frank noticed Geoff Lukens standing on the curb. "Good morning, Frank. Great service today, wasn't it? I thought the choir was especially good."

"Yes, that hymn has always been a favorite of mine," Frank said, adding, "But I suspect you didn't wait around just to remark on the choir."

"True. I shouldn't do this at church, I know," Geoff said, lowering his voice to a whisper. "But I wanted to give you and Louanne a heads up."

"I'm hoping you are about to say that our loan was approved, but by the look on your face, I'm guessing I would be wrong about that."

"Frank, Loon's Nest closed very abruptly in 1974 and hasn't been operated since then. It's a concern."

"We were completely open about that the first time we talked to you—what's changed?"

Geoff spoke, "I know, I know. But questions have come up about the 'Why?' of it all. Why did it close down so suddenly in 1974? Why did no one open it up again? Why didn't Louanne's family sell it years ago if no one planned to operate it? My VP wants some of these questions answered before we can proceed." Geoff clapped Frank on the shoulder and concluded, "The good news is, they are not outright denying the loan. Just tabling a decision pending some more answers."

******

June 11, 2014

Emily stood by the kitchen window at her parents' house waiting for the tall older brother of her high school friend to pull into the driveway. Just last week she'd confided to her mother about the secret crush she'd had on him throughout high school. She hadn't seen him in ten years and now he was coming to help her parents realize a dream. As soon as she saw the car, she touched up her lipstick, smoothed her hair and walked slowly to the door to greet him.

"Thank you for coming, Deion. My parents really appreciated your help last week. Now that the bank says we need more answers, we just don't know what to do. My brother Robby and I are here to see if we can help. Luke and Sid had to work," Emily spoke far too quickly as she ushered Deion into the family room.

Louanne greeted Deion and offered everyone lemonade before taking a seat next to Frank on the sofa. Robby and Deion sat in the two Queen Anne chairs and Emily perched on the ottoman looking a little like a cat waiting for a mouse to pounce upon. Two large cardboard boxes were in the middle of the floor and several old photo albums were laid across the coffee table.

"We've searched and searched through all the papers and albums we found in the attic at the family cottage at the lake," Louanne began. "We can't find a thing that helps answer any of the bank's questions. I've spoken to my cousin Chris and he swears up and down that he doesn't know anything either."

"And everyone else in the family associated with the campground in 1974 is dead," Frank said. "We're at a loss as to what to do next."

"You could hire a private investigator to get to the bottom of the story. I brought a few names of investigators our firm has worked with. These guys are reputable," Deion handed Louanne a sheet of paper with names, phone numbers and websites.

"Oh look, Frank, this one, Livingston Investigations, they are based over in Sweetland where my friends Homer and Celia Evers live. Wonder if they know these folks?"

"That will take some time, of course," Deion continued, "And I gather there is some urgency here to move things forward."

"Yes, Lou's cousin needs his share of the proceeds before school starts in September," Frank explained.

"Right, I remember that from our last discussion. So, I suggest that even if you do go ahead with the investigator, we strategize a few additional steps. We may not be able to get the exact answers the bank is seeking, but we can get them some information that should help assuage their fears."

"Really, Deion? What would that involve?" Emily spoke for the first time.

"What the bank really needs to know is if the mysterious history of the campground will impact sales today, in 2014. We can learn this two ways. First, we need to go up there to Loonstone Lake. Talk to people in the community. Perhaps conduct a focus group meeting or at least a series of interviews."

"And what is the second thing?" Robby asked.

"I know your cousin had the property appraised, but we should hire our own appraiser and inspector to thoroughly assess the property. Make sure there is nothing there that would hinder the successful execution of your business plan."

"I'm guessing you have some recommendations for that as well?" Louanne asked, holding her hand out expectantly.

******

"Look at this one, mommy is this you?" Emily held an old black and white photo in her hands. After Deion left and Robby left, Frank had stepped out to mow the lawn, but mother and daughter lingered in the living room looking through the old family photos and documents one more time.

"Oh my," Louanne laughed at the photo of a cute baby sitting in a bucket next to a large dog. "Yes, that's me, and that's Ramy and Popi's dog, Stinker. I was terrified of him—look at my face!" By now both women were rolling with laughter.

"Mom? Do you really think Deion's plan will work? I'm dying to know what really happened in 1974, but even more, I want you and dad to be able to have your dream."

"I guess it's in God's hands now," Louanne said, "But one thing is for sure, it looks like we'll get to spend some more time with

Deion, and from the looks of things, that means we'll get to spend some more time with you, too!"

Chapter Five

July 11, 2014

"Pull over, right here," Louanne said to her husband as they approached the turn-off for Loon's Nest Campground. She reached into the back of the van and retrieved the bunch of yellow balloons tied to the armrest. "You go on ahead, I'll walk the rest of the way."

Louanne tied the balloons to a tree and began the three-quarter mile walk to camp. Breathing in the balsam-scented air, she pinched herself to make sure this day had really arrived. What a roller-coaster the past month had been, but with the help of Deion, Geoff, family, friends and a boatload of prayer, the day had finally come to start whipping Loon's Nest into shape before the grand opening. She relished these few quiet moments before the vehicles filled with volunteers would begin arriving.

"Cleaning supplies, check. Food to feed an army, and charcoal for the grill, check. Enough gas for the lawn-movers and other yard equipment, check." Louanne began rehearsing her checklist aloud as she walked towards camp. She was just steps away from the main entrance when a motorcycle roared past her and spun around in the dirt stopping in front of her. Stepping down and removing their helmets, the driver and his passenger burst out laughing.

"Deion and Emily, you about gave me a heart attack! You didn't say you'd be arriving on a Harley!" Louanne did her best to look annoyed, but her heart was bursting with joy to see her Emily so happy. She and Deion had become an "item" ever since the trip to Loon Lake for the community focus groups. Although that was only three weeks ago, they were already the kind of couple that finishes one another's sentences. Louanne couldn't help but dream about wedding bells in the future.

"I took the bike Mrs. H because my brother DeMonte is driving my dad's truck up here with all the paints and ladders we bought with the money donated by Sigma Pi Phi. He should be here soon," Deion said just as Frank emerged from the family cottage to join the conversation.

"What an outpouring of blessings we've received. From your fraternity, Em's employer and several churches and youth groups—

we are going to be cookin' with bacon grease here soon," Frank said, clapping Deion heartily on the back.

Just then a convoy of four vehicles began pulling into the driveway led by Deion's brother DeMonte. Next came sweet little Rozene Gentry with an SUV full of girls from the Youth Acres Group home down in Sweetland. Louanne had met them recently while visiting her college roommate, Celia Evers. Rick Ellison's van filled with men from the Danville Rotary club was next and Louanne's sister Karen pulled up the rear with her family.

Louanne watched, her mouth agape, as people, coolers, cleaning supplies and cans of paint spilled out of all vehicles and the parking area began buzzing with reunions and introductions. She and Frank walked around greeting each person, thanking them for coming to the special "Loon's Nest Clean-Up Weekend" and welcoming the newcomers as they arrived. By the time Luke, Sid and Liam pulled in a few minutes later, six different groups of volunteers were ready to get to work.

Emily pulled out her camp whistle and called the crowd to order. With all of her experience during college and in her current job organizing volunteer crews for service projects, she was the perfect person to whip this group into shape. "We have four primary projects," she began, "yard work, painting, interior cleaning and minor repairs. Big repairs, plumbing and such were completed last week, so all of the big systems are in tip-top shape and you'll see we have a brand-new, up-to-code kitchen in the dining hall across the road. After the interior cleaning is finished, we have a fifth project—bed making and pillow fluffing." That drew a laugh.

"Each project has a crew leader," She continued. "I'll introduce you to the leaders and then, depending upon which project you are most interested in, you gather with the crew leader and that's where you will get further instructions and necessary supplies. Rick Ellison from Danville is in charge of the yard crew. If you want to do yard work, meet him in front of the shed over there."

"Don't let Robby get in that line!" Luke called out, ribbing his younger brother. "He's dangerous around lawnmowers—remember the time he cut his toe off?" This drew gasps and another round of laughter before Emily could continue.

"Dean Withers and DeMonte Abernathy from Sigma Pi Phi are co-leading the painting crew. There will be both inside and outside painting jobs—meet them by the white tent over there if you want to paint," Emily said and continued until all leaders had been introduced and everyone had dispersed to their chosen crew. Looking up from her checklist, she noticed an overweight teenager leaning against a tree, alone. "I'm Emily, what's your name?" she asked, walking up to him.

"Kevin," he mumbled.

"Can't find a crew that interests you?"

"I came with my youth group cuz the pastor said I should come. But I ain't no good at any of this stuff. I'm in foster care so I ain't allowed to use lawnmowers, and if I paint, I'd just make a mess."

"Forget about the mess part, is painting something you'd like to do?" Emily asked and watched the boy's eyes light up just a bit as he slowly nodded. "Super, I know there is a paint job you can do. We need the whole backside of the dining hall painted. I need someone big and strong like you to work on that. Would you be willing to give it a try? I'll make sure you have a couple helpers, you won't be alone."

"Really? You gonna trust me with a paint brush?"

"I sure will. Ready to start? Let's walk over so you can meet Dean and DeMonte and they'll get you set up."

After Emily made sure Dean welcomed Kevin, she strolled over to where her mother and Luke were setting up a refreshment tent and getting the charcoal grill started. "Mom, I have to tell you about this boy Kevin I just met. He's exactly the kind of kid dad wants to bring here to Loon's Nest. The campground isn't even open yet and dad's dream is already starting to come true. It gave me goosebumps."

"Our God is a God of goosebumps and muscle-grease," Louanne said, looking around. "Just look at all these people who showed up to help. I can hardly take it in. I do hope I planned enough food."

"Mom. Seriously. Have you ever not planned enough food? For anything?" Luke affectionately elbowed his mom in the ribs, adding, "but they aren't going to want it raw, so let's get cooking."

******

July 13, 2014

Louanne plopped down on the couch and laid her feet across Frank's lap, a not-too-subtle hint that she was ready for a foot rub. In the distance, she could hear the loons begin their evening serenade. What an exhausting, but exhilarating, weekend it had been. Loon's Nest looked like it had received a total makeover and was now the belle of the ball. "I can't wait for Chris, Janey and Brian to see it when they come next weekend for the official 'christening!'" she said to Frank as he began kneading her aching feet.

"They won't recognize it at all. I can't remember when I have ever witnessed such a transformation. I can hardly wait to see all the roots and wings that will sprout here over the next few years."

"Me either," Louanne said, closing her eyes and leaning her head back on a small grey pillow. "My only disappointment is that those private investigators didn't get us any closer to the truth about what happened in 1974. I know the bank accepted the information we gave them, but as for me, I need to keep looking for answers. I can't abide an unsolved mystery, Frank Hubert, I just can't."

Roots & Wings at Loonstone Lake

Volume One - Call of the Loons

Recipes

Louanne's Shrimp & Avocado Salad

Ingredients

2 limes, juiced, plus additional lime wedges for garnish
1 clove garlic diced
1 tablespoon olive oil
1 pound shrimp cooked, peeled, de-veined and chopped
1 medium tomato diced
1 avocado diced
1 red bell pepper diced
1 red onion diced
1 tablespoon cilantro chopped
Salt and pepper to taste
Romaine or Bibb lettuce finely chopped

Directions

1. Combine lime juice, garlic and olive oil in a bowl.
2. Add shrimp and stir to coat all shrimp pieces with lime juice mixture.
3. Add tomato, avocado, red bell pepper and red onion, stir again.
4. Add cilantro, salt and pepper, toss gently.
5. Make a bed of chopped lettuce in a pretty salad bowl
6. Top with shrimp and avocado mixture, garnish with a few wedges of lime. Serve chilled.

Pucker-up Punch

Ingredients:

10 lemons, juiced (you should have about 2 cups of juice)
1.5 cups of sugar
1 cup boiling water
7 cups cold water
1 cup unsweetened cranberry juice
2 cups seltzer water
Optional: 3 scoops of lemon, lime or raspberry sherbet

Directions:

1. Make simple syrup by mixing sugar and boiling water until sugar is completely dissolved. Set aside to cool.
2. When simple syrup has cooled, add lemon juice and stir until thoroughly mixed.
3. Pour lemon juice mixture, cold water, and cranberry juice into a punch bowl.
4. Slowly add seltzer water.
5. If desired, add 3 scoops of sherbet.

Fiesta Chicken Packets

Ingredients:

4 boneless, skinless chicken thighs or breasts
2 limes, juiced
2 tablespoons olive oil
1 15 ounce can black beans, drained
2 cups corn—can be frozen, canned or scraped off the cob
2 tomatoes, seeded and diced
2 tablespoons finely diced jalapenos or green chilies
1 clove garlic, finely diced
1 teaspoon Adobo seasoning
1 teaspoon red pepper flakes
1 teaspoon chili powder
Salt and pepper to taste
Optional: ½ cup shredded Pepper-Jack cheese and ½ cup sour cream

Directions:

1. Prepare and preheat your outdoor grill—this recipe works with a wood-based campfire, charcoal or gas grill.
2. Combine lime juice and olive oil in a bowl, add chicken thighs or breasts, toss to coat and set aside to marinate for at least 30 minutes.
3. Combine black beans, corn, tomatoes and jalapenos in a bowl.
4. Add garlic and all seasonings, stir.
5. Lay four squares of heavy-duty aluminum foil on the counter; spray each sheet of foil with cooking spray.
6. Place one chicken thigh or breast in the center of each sheet of foil.
7. Spoon a quarter of the corn and bean mixture on top of each piece of chicken.
8. Bring up sides of foil and fold to make a secure packet.
9. Place packets on grill. Grill approximately 20 minutes until chicken is no longer pink in the middle. Actual time may vary depending on the specific type of grill you use.
10. *Optional: Before serving add 1/8 cup of shredded cheese and a dollop of sour cream to each serving.*

Note: This recipe may also be made in an oven. Preheat oven to 450 degrees. Place chicken packets on a baking sheet and cook for 15-20 minutes.

New England Baked Beans

Ingredients

1 pound dry great northern or navy beans
8 cups water
2 yellow onions, cut into chunks
8 ounces salt pork, cut into cubes
½ cup Vermont Maple Syrup, Grade B
¼ cup dark molasses or dark brown sugar
3-4 cups boiling water
¼ cup ketchup
¼ cup apple cider
2 tablespoons yellow mustard
Salt and Pepper to taste

Directions

1. Place beans in a large pot, add water, and bring to a boil. Boil for 5 minutes and remove from heat.
2. Let beans set for 1 hour and then drain.
3. Preheat oven to 250 degrees
4. Using an old-fashioned bean pot or a Dutch oven, line the bottom with the salt pork and onion chunks
5. Add beans, maple syrup, molasses (or brown sugar) and stir
6. Pour 3-4 cups boiling water over beans and cover tightly
7. Bake for 3 hours stirring occasionally.
8. Remove from oven, uncover beans, add ketchup, apple cider, mustard, salt and pepper and stir.
9. Bake for 3 more hours, stirring occasionally.
10. When stirring if necessary you may add small amounts of additional water, a few tablespoons at a time.
11. Serve with brown bread or corn bread.

Cricket Pie

Ingredients:

1 Oreo piecrust
1 package of Oreo or similar sandwich cookies
1 pint coffee ice cream, softened
1 cup heavy cream, whipped plus additional whipped cream for garnish

Directions:

1. Break cookies into small (bite-size) chunks, reserve approximately one fourth of the cookie chunks.
2. Mix all but reserved cookie chunks into softened ice cream, stir.
3. Fold whipped cream into ice cream mixture,
4. Place ice cream mixture into piecrust.
5. Scatter reserved cookie chunks on top of pie.
6. Freeze.
7. Serve with dollops of whipped cream.

www.ingramcontent.com/pod-product-compliance
Lightning Source LLC
Chambersburg PA
CBHW071623040426
42452CB00009B/1457